Can't Dia.beat.us

The Highs and Lows of Raising a Type 1 Diabetic Child

To Laura
With love!

By:

Trina Licavoli Gunzel

Cover design and artwork by Trina Licavoli Gunzel

Published by

Best Educators, LLC.

Branson, MO

www.besteducators.com

www.trinagunzel.com

www.jongunzel.com

www.type1family.com

Disclaimer: This is not a technical resource book. This is a real life 24-7 biographical and self help book from and for people who want to know more about how to overcome challenges and thrive, not just survive a Type 1 life. Nothing in this book is meant to replace your recommended medical program and treatment. It is an educational resource and a behind the scenes look at a Type 1 Diabetic Family.

ISBN-13:
978-1519233851

Library of Congress Control Number: 2015919221 CreateSpace Independent Publishing Platform, North Charleston, SC

DEDICATION

To my son Wyatt, the sweetest and strongest person I know. I love you and enjoy being your Mama! I hope you'll always know how grateful we are for you and how much you mean to us.

To all those who live a life with Type 1 Diabetes every day, you are not alone.

With love, Trina Licavoli Gunzel

A special thank you to my husband, Jon, my best friend, a wonderful father to our children, and our own in house, on-call, Type 1 Family Specialist. I couldn't have written this without your love and support. I appreciate you, the cool title you came up with, and your valuable input.

To our little ray of sunshine, Abbie Rose, you were our biggest surprise and greatest blessing! Thank you for being so helpful and cheerful.

CONTENTS

FORWARD

The Untold Story

If you are taking the time to read this, I know you are someone who is curious about the lives of Type 1 Diabetics and I appreciate you wanting to know more. Maybe you are a Type 1 Diabetic and just want to connect with someone else or laugh at some of the humorous times, too. Maybe you just want to know that everyone has their own personal struggles and see some examples of how to live with whatever happens in your life's journey. Honestly, this is not a story I ever wanted to write or thought I would have anything specific to share that could help people involving blood, needles, carb counting, and sleepless nights.

I am writing this story to honor all of the people who live and who have died waiting for a cure for Type 1 Diabetes and for all of their friends, family, and medical professionals who have been by their side encouraging and supporting them. As the mother of a Type 1 Diabetic child, it is my constant prayer and hope there will be a cure. I hope that sharing our story will spread awareness and give people an insight to the true highs and lows of a

Type 1 Diabetic life. This is not a medical textbook and is not meant to replace your recommended treatment program. It is heart breaking, humorous, encouraging, and courageous life journey. Attending the DYF's Camp Bearskin Meadow changed our life. I hope to be able to sponsor many Type 1 Diabetic families so they can attend this life saving camp, through portions of my book sales.

Being a Type 1 Mom has grown my strength, endurance, tested and grown my faith, and shown me that no matter what life throws our way, we can overcome it with great effort and great love. I appreciate you wanting to know our story and if we can pay our family's learning and love forward to help others understand, see how to overcome struggles, and not feel alone in whatever they are going through, there has been a much bigger purpose for our pain. #THRIVE, don't just survive in this life. You were made for more!

With love,

Trina Licavoli Gunzel

Chapter 1

The Sweet Factor

My husband, Jon, and I tried for seven years to have a child before finally giving up and resigning ourselves to the fact that we would just be the best aunt and uncle ever for our nieces and nephews. Not being able to have children was a hard pill for us to swallow, but of course that is when God finally said, "Yes!" and we began our journey of expecting our first child. I was teaching full time and setting up the Structured English Immersion Program in my school district.

It was a very busy time in my career and severe morning sickness made the first three months extra challenging. I had almost finished the school year and we seemed to be all set up for the natural childbirth plan we'd hoped for. Specifically, I remember Jon and I going to our birthing class and listening to the nurse share delivery statistics. One of us in the group would probably need to have a cesarean delivery. We elbowed each other and teased that would never be us. My mom had six children, all natural births, so I was extremely confident in my birth plan. But, however unlikely or how confident we were, we were going to be that statistic.

I was feeling great and planned on finishing out the school year since I wasn't due until the end of May or early June. The day that changed, I was outside waiting for my class to line up from recess when a student accidently slipped on the gravel playground and knocked me down. It was completely unexpected and we both fell all the way to the ground. I landed on my side when I fell and the injury caused me to go right into early labor. They were able to stop the contractions at the hospital to buy our bun a little more time in the oven, but a few weeks later, it was go time. Our baby had turned when I fell so, although we tried for a week to get him to turn head down for delivery, he was head up and wedged under my ribs which meant I now had to have a c-section delivery. My statistical improbability was now my unfortunate reality.

I remember having to sign some papers that were pretty intimidating before getting my spinal block and holding my son. Actually, I asked the doctor, "Well, do I have another option? I mean, you're not really giving me much of a choice here, right?" At first, I was really frustrated and disappointed I had to have surgery, but then decided that, either way, I was just happy and thankful our little miracle was born. I was so grateful that we were both safe and healthy and will never forget the day I first laid eyes on my precious son.

We had been calling him Wyatt for months and when my husband called out his name, he actually turned his little head toward his daddy. It was such an awesome moment! Well, I know I am not the first parent who's ever said this, but, our son Wyatt was absolutely perfect! He was a ray of sunshine and melted our hearts from the moment we first met. Being the first grandchild on both sides of the family, he had all the makings of the "Sweet Factor" that any child could have.

The Sweet Factor is what I'm calling the ability to charm everyone you meet, the perfect balance of charisma, intelligence, strength, endurance, and a feeling that bigger things in life are just destined for a person. We felt a tremendous responsibility raising a child that made friends everywhere we went and who people were just naturally drawn to. There was no part of Wyatt that was the tiniest bit shy or unwilling to talk to or help anyone. He had the Sweet Factor from head to toe and made friends everywhere we took him. For us, in all ways, we really felt our life was complete and knew we were beyond blessed. Raising a child is a lot of work, but we had great support from family and friends since we moved back to our hometown in Arizona. We were absolutely set up for success!

Looking back now, I can see that was all part of God's plan and I am thankful we had a place that really knew and embraced the concept "it takes a village to raise a child" with what was headed our way.

#Lesson 1: Plan for the unexpected:

Reflection Opportunity:

Think about a time in your life when you thought you had everything all figured out and had to completely change your plan. How can you be more prepared for things that are out of your control? You might not be able to prevent certain things that happen to you in your life, but do you have great friends you can talk to about it? Do you have an outlet for stress or a way to be encouraged? Can you see that things you go through are part of your personal life journey and accept that you might have to go through specific situations in order to learn and grow?

I have found there was nothing I could do to prevent certain situations in my life, but by having a great support group of people and positive outlets, it made things more possible. This is my plan for whatever unexpected thing comes my way next: Try hard and proceed with love. Take a few minutes to reflect and journal that experience in a notebook or share it on my Facebook author page: Trina Licavoli Gunzel.

Chapter 2

A Pre Type 1 Diabetic Life

I remember one day, standing in my classroom thinking, I really love all of these children and enjoy teaching them every day, but how can I use all of my education and training here, and not do what I know in my heart is best for MY OWN child? I was an excellent teacher and passionate about helping others, but every day I left my son, my heart just broke a little more.

My husband was wonderful caring for him, growing our photography business, and coaching, but I still wanted to be there. I would get up early and pump breast milk twice before work so that he could supplement that with formula during the day, but I was uncomfortably engorged when I got home. Balancing "the breast feeding while working thing" was anything but easy for me. Many mothers had shared their stories with me about trying to juggle their career needs, financially, with the desire to stay home and raise their baby and I was now forced with the same dilemma. Have you ever experienced that torn heart situation? I really had to weigh all the options, but in the end, I had to resign and put my best effort into raising my son. I knew my career would always be there for me, but felt these toddler years would go so quickly, I didn't want to miss them.

I am the type of person who tries to live my life with no regrets. Living this way means I don't have a bucket list to do later. I choose to live my life now and be at peace with my decisions, knowing I did the best I could with what I have, TODAY. Embracing that attitude, we sold our house, downsized, and had taken our photography business to a level that allowed me to quit my teaching job, join my husband, AND help raise our son. I continued to do educational training, consulting, and writing on the side and together, we made it work.

Those first four years of our son's life were something we will treasure forever. Our new move allowed us to be close to Roosevelt Lake and my husband started doing fishing guiding, as well. We traveled the country fishing tournaments, doing photo shoots, and doing educational trainings and workshops. Wyatt was such a great traveler and since we had him on the boat since he was eight days old, he was as comfortable on the water as he was off. He was such a sweet and smart little boy and everyone who knows him would say the same. I remember he would come into my room and ask me if I wanted to watch the sunrise with him. He had a fisherman's blood and internal alarm clock that seemed to literally rise and set with the sun. We had many wonderful picnics, hiking trips, road trips, visits with family, and he was an integral part of our photo team. Many of our customers would request him because he would make their child laugh and then my husband would capture that true joyful smile.

Getting to work from home, build our business as a family, and enjoy the great outdoors was a dream come true! As parents, we really felt our life was complete and while we thought about having more children, we had a few miscarriages that made us feel that we were so fortunate to have our son, we'd better just stop while we were ahead.

#Lesson 2: Enjoy the moment:

Reflection Opportunity:

Think about a time in your life that was just pure joy. Take some time to write down a specific memory about a period in your life you really enjoyed. Being able to express gratitude for that time and have it to look back on will be a great source of positive energy for you to draw upon during more challenging times. Take a few minutes to reflect and journal that experience in a notebook or share it on my Facebook author page: Trina Licavoli Gunzel.

Chapter 3
The Wondering Phase

Wyatt was a healthy baby. He had occasional illnesses, but usually got better quickly. In the spring before he was diagnosed, he got pneumonia. I seem to also remember him getting a red rash that would move around his body when he was sick, and then go away after about two weeks. Over that same summer, he didn't want to eat very much. He had always been a great eater, so this was odd for him. His stomach also seemed distended and he was extremely constipated. Looking back at pictures, he appears kind of puffy in his face.

My mother's instincts knew something wasn't right with my son and we had repeated visits to our doctor who sent us for all sorts of tests to try to diagnose the problem. He suspected some type of tumor or even cancer, but nothing showed up on any scans. This was so frustrating but NOTHING ever showed up. Eventually, he started to improve, and without any positive test results, we were just advised to bring him in if anything changed. Life returned to normal for a while.

Preschool started and that was exciting! Wyatt was four and had been potty trained since he was two. That fall, he started wetting the bed and couldn't hold it when we were out, crying that he had to go to the bathroom. We'd have to pull over on the side of the road commuting to photo shoots and run into restrooms for him. It didn't make any sense. He was drinking constantly so we thought maybe he was just drinking too much. We also kept asking our doctor about bladder infections, but those never showed up either. I remember noticing sometimes that his urine would be frothy and have bubbles in it and I questioned him about drinking bath soap. I thought that was odd, but it wasn't consistent. Our doctor even tested Wyatt's blood sugar levels and nothing appeared out of the ordinary.

Then, the week before Thanksgiving, Wyatt went into diabetic ketoacidosis. I'll never forget that day. My cousin picked him up from pre-school since we were at work, and when I went to get him, he was just resting on the sofa. He seemed like he might have been coming down with some respiratory illness and didn't really seem like himself. I remember sleeping on the floor in his room that night, so I could listen to him breathe. He was breathing pretty hard, but he didn't have a fever, so it seemed like some form of respiratory cold.

The next morning, I was doing conference calls for my online class and noticed my son started to slouch over in the chair. He was watching a show and just didn't look right. I called my principal and told her I had to take my son to the doctor because he was sick and we took Wyatt immediately in. Our doctor was concerned and got our son right in because he had been suspecting something, although nothing had showed up on any test results. When he saw Wyatt he diagnosed him immediately with diabetic ketoacidosis (DKA) and called the hospital to admit him. Google Ketoacidosis Explanation and Signs to look for, to find more specific information. The heavy-labored, uncontrollable, fast breathing was our red flag indicator.

Nobody at the hospital could believe our son had Type 1 Diabetes and they were shocked when his blood test came back over 900. We were taken by ambulance to a larger hospital that was able to treat him and began the process of slowly having our son come back from a diabetic induced coma. It was the worst 5 days of our lives trying to learn how to take care of our son before we were allowed to take him home. We had to overcome OUR fear of blood, needles, and learn how to calculate carbs and insulin doses for a CHILD AFRAID of shots and needles. In order to live, he now had to have shots, combined with finger pokes and doses, about 12 times per day. We couldn't picture how this new reality was ever going to result in a happy family or even possible life.

It is now 7 years later and we have come a long way since that day, but we still live with high and low blood sugars that are just a part of this autoimmune disease, until there is a cure. We do the best we can helping our son and want him to know how much he is loved and supported. The everyday management of Type 1 Diabetes is intense and constant. People living with it need your support, love, and understanding. Many try not to let it stop them from doing anything, but there is extra care needed, especially for extreme exercise, eating, sleeping, doses, and well...pretty much everything. It is a life changing and life threatening condition that, if not diagnosed and treated properly, is a silent killer. People can look fine and appear "healthy" while their organs are being damaged on the inside.

My heart and prayers go out to all the families who have lost someone to Type 1 Diabetes. I hope sharing our story will increase awareness and add to the understanding of this silent autoimmune disease. To all those who live it and love someone with it every day, my prayers are with you for strength and courage. You are not alone!

#Lesson 3: Be aware:

Reflection Opportunity:

Is there anything health wise that you have been noticing that you are concerned about? Do you need to make the time to take care of yourself or someone you love? Whatever it is, diet, exercise, a spot or pain you need to get checked out, make taking care of that a priority. There are so many times that if we could eliminate the worry or stress about something by just treating it, we would improve greatly.

Whatever your resource for healing is, praying, alternative medicine, traditional, or natural healing practices, I pray you will take good care of yourself and live your life to the fullest. Take some time to journal what health issues you will address.

Chapter 4
The Shock Wave

It's important to address the post hospital life for a full understanding of how this condition changes everything. After we brought Wyatt home from the hospital, we were absolutely numb. It seemed like we would never recover from this. We had phone messages for our business we didn't even want to return and minute by minute seemed to be taken up with carbohydrate calculations, insulin doses, our son crying because he wanted to eat something and we didn't know what to feed him, and a completely exhausted and shattered family.

It was the week of Thanksgiving and although my parents had invited us to go to their house, we felt that we were in NO WAY prepared to travel or to be able to figure out all of the insulin doses we would need to know in order to take Wyatt to a meal out, anywhere. We were simply overwhelmed with our situation. Although Wyatt was four years old, we felt like we had a complete newborn again and were all having to overcome our fear of blood and needles every three hours.

Have you had those periods in your life where you just needed someone to reach in and give you a little understanding and help, but you couldn't even explain what you needed? My parents have always been great at knowing and doing exactly what was needed in situations like that.

I'll never forget…it was quiet in our house in Tonto Basin early that Thursday morning. We had puffy eyes and were awake listening to the birds and watching the sun stream in through the windows. Wyatt just wanted to be cuddled on the couch and we'd just gone through a huge crying episode. We had to check his tiny finger to get a drop of blood for his glucose meter and had to give him an insulin shot so he could have his sippy cup of milk. This joyous morning routine had turned into a frustrating event and it wasn't taking our son long to figure out that he might just try "not eating" so he didn't have to get shots anymore.

He finally opted for the milk and got a shot anyway and was settling down watching his favorite program, *The Wonder Pets*. We weren't even thinking about Thanksgiving, but my Dad didn't want his grandson (and us) to miss it and thought the smell of a home cooked stuffed turkey roasting in our own oven on the holiday might be a comfort to us. Instead of only making a turkey for himself and the rest of the family, he stuffed a second turkey and drove it to our house, an hour away, and came to put it in our oven.

I was brought to tears and we were so overwhelmed and happily surprised when we heard him knock at the door holding a roasting pan. He also brought some homemade pumpkin pie, the carbohydrate amounts he'd written down, and gave us much needed healing hugs after just returning from the hospital. He didn't stay long, but my Dad making that over the top effort to reach out and show us love when we desperately needed it meant the world to us.

My husband's favorite food is my Dad's homemade stuffing so Dad to Dad, sometimes reaching out like that is just an extra way to show you care and that you actually are able to do something for someone at a time when you feel otherwise helpless. I don't remember the specific advice he told Wyatt, but I know it included something about him being brave and letting him know how much he was loved. Getting hugs from my Dad made me feel like this was going to be possible and I knew that we weren't alone.

#Lesson 4: Be grateful:

Reflection Opportunity:

Have you ever had someone do something for you that you wanted to thank but haven't taken the time to? Today, write a letter to someone you want to thank or send them an e-mail. If you can't reach them, write in your journal some things you are thankful for. Keep those experiences to refer to when you're having hard days and let your attitude of gratitude recharge your heart.

Chapter 5

The Blame Game

Can I just say that the first months adjusting to raising a Type 1 Diabetic child were NOT easy! Maybe they are for some people, but it challenged us in every way possible. I still want to scream when I think about them!

Somehow, we tried to put back together some version of our previous life. Managing two different required insulin shots daily and calculating carbohydrates for every meal and snack was completely intimidating, yet HAD to be done. Work had to go on, meal time had to go on, but nothing was the same.

Suddenly, things that were quick, like feeding my son a snack, took an hour. I also remember a phase of buying prepackaged food because it seemed easier since the carbohydrate counts were spelled out, instead of trying to cook the homemade recipes I used to make from scratch. I hated that I didn't feel like I was able to feed my child healthy anymore and was depending on someone else figuring out the carbohydrate amounts.

It was the most paralyzing and frustrating time of my life. I mean, come on, feeding your kid? That had always seemed like the most basic necessary thing we were able to do for him. Now, Wyatt didn't even want food because he didn't want another shot. Something that was once pure joy now was a fight for EVERY MEAL. I really didn't know how we were going to survive this.

Then, came all of the reasons EVERYONE EVERYWHERE we went wanted to tell us was the cause of our son getting Type 1 Diabetes. This is where I have to look at this with a grain of salt because while I can laugh at it now, it was absolutely so frustrating to have to listen to and stomach from people who, I'm sure, had good intentions, but just added to our frustration. So, for this part, I am just going to make a list of the Top 10 Things you should never say to your Type 1 friends and family are the cause of their child getting diagnosed. I'll reinforce it for effect:

Top 10 Things you should never say to your Type 1 friends and family are the cause of their child getting diagnosed:

1. They ate too much candy.

2. They didn't exercise enough.
3. They drank milk.
4. They ate too much fruit.
5. It's because the parents are going to get Type 2 Diabetes that their child got it.
6. Because God knew they could handle it.
7. Because they sinned so they are being punished.
8. That their child is suffering to pay for something they did.
9. Because they drank soda.
10. Because their child was always sick.

None of these reasons help. Playing the blame game and trying to point fingers out as to who caused it or identify the reason for their child getting Type 1 Diabetes does NOT show support.

The flip side view: Empathizing with Type 1 children and their families and offering support they need, CAN help. They need to know they are loved. They need people to understand they are hurting and trying their best. If you want to really help, share specific technology advances or studies that work toward a cure or advancements, learn how to help care for their child so they can have a date night or break, help them financially if you are able since the medical costs and daily care is outrageous, pray for them, listen to them, have a loving and compassionate heart for their situation, and share camp ideas and day to day survival tips from other Type 1 families.

If you have resources, alternative program ideas, or food suggestions, you can see if they would like them. But, you will need to consider your timing and realize they have just been hammered with a MAJOR shock wave and had to go through Type 1 boot camp just to get their kid out of the hospital. If they aren't receptive initially, it's probably because they have more information than the five minutes you just spent googling Type 1 Diabetes and it was under intense learning conditions. Honestly, they will probably be grateful for more resources soon, but unless you are a trained endocrinologist, nurse, or person willing to go through the training hand in hand with them so they can take a nap, they might snap when you offer a "cure." They have just been shown there isn't one yet, and there probably isn't even the reality of one heading their way fast enough to meet their immediate needs.

The fact is, for some unknown reason, their child's body attacked itself, their pancreas stopped producing insulin, and they almost died. Every day, every hour, every minute is now a balancing act to play "artificial pancreas" with the available resources to still help their child live and it is a constant, life threatening condition. Rather than blaming, work to help find solutions, learn how to help them care for their child so they have someone else who can help, and most of all, listen and respect the way they want to talk about it and how they choose to live their lives with it.

I suppose it is only natural when challenging things happen to look for the cause of it, but it isn't that simple. For our son, even if we could dial in the exact cause…did it really matter? How would that change anything? We participate in the Trial Net Studies every year and to date; neither my husband, myself, nor our daughter has the gene structure that would indicate we would have a Type 1 Diabetic child. Whatever the reason is that our son was diagnosed, we are hoping our story will inspire, encourage, and enlighten others in this 24-7 blood glucose monitoring and intense management world. If by being an open book to the everyday reality of a Type 1 life, a cure is pushed faster or others feel like they have been heard, we are trying to share for those reasons. This is really an untold story and the blinders need to be taken off so the depth of what it does to families can really be known.

#Lesson 5: The Blame Game:

Reflection Opportunity:

Think about a time in your life where you were blamed for something that wasn't your fault. What emotions did that cause you to feel? What could have happened in that situation that would have helped you feel more understood? Work to show empathy to others and make sure you have all the facts in the future before making judgment on others. Take a few minutes to reflect and journal that experience in a notebook or share it on my Facebook author page: Trina Licavoli Gunzel.

Chapter 6

Insulin Man - The Super Hero For Type 1 Kids

The day "Insulin Man" came to life was the day I was racking my tired brain trying to figure out a way to makes shots "fun" for my four year old. Can you imagine? Take a minute and picture yourself in my shoes. I have this amazing, adorable little boy who loves airplanes, cars, fishing, and pretty much anything that flies. He also used to be the kind of kid who would eat anything and was a pretty athletic little dude.

It didn't take him long to figure out, after he was diagnosed, that he needed to get a shot every time he ate. So, his little mind put together that if he just didn't eat, he could eliminate a bunch of shots. Well, you can see right away how that was not going to work. He was tired and hungry and wanted something to eat. We'd made some food choices and I was getting ready to give him his insulin shot for the meal when he completely *wigged out*. I mean, he was not going to let me give him a shot for ANYTHING! So, our often real life hero, my husband, found this wonderful tool called Inject-ease that I could actually put a syringe into and then it hid the needle.

This made the situation seem more possible for my son, who was afraid of needles, and myself, who was trying to overcome my fear of needles as fast as I could to help him. We were definitely in that super heroes faze with shows and I decided to tell Wyatt that there was a Super Hero just for Type 1 Diabetics. He stopped crying for a minute and looked at me with a pretty serious face. "What's his name?" he asked. I pulled out a little felt man with a blindfold on who was wearing a blue and white super suit. I slid him over the Inject-ease loaded cartridge and told him that Insulin Man showed up to help all the kids with Type 1 Diabetes be brave so they wouldn't be afraid of needles anymore. I shared that he would come and stay as long as Wyatt needed him to, then he would fly off and help another child who was afraid of needles.

Wyatt seemed to think it was pretty cool that Insulin Man had insulin that came out of his head that gave him *Super Power Juice* to make his body get the energy he needed from the food. Insulin Man helped Wyatt decide to eat that day and he stayed around for a few months before flying off to help another family. I was praying for a solution to help my little boy and this little super hero transformed our house from a teary tragedy every meal time to a place where my little boy wanted to eat again. He was able to overcome his fear of needles (and me too!) so we could inject the insulin he needed to live. Step by step…we decided we were going to overcome these fears and transform them into victories!

#Lesson 6: Your Super Hero:

Reflection Opportunity:

If you could invent a Super Hero to help you overcome a fear or to help someone you know overcome something they are struggling with, what would it be? What would the Super Hero's name be, what would they do, and what would they look like? How could this make a positive change? Take a few minutes to reflect and journal that experience in a notebook or share your ideas on my Facebook author page: Trina Licavoli Gunzel.

Chapter 7

One Prick At A Time Is Enough

As part of sharing our story, there are lots of highs and lows that happen daily and will continue to. We have come to embrace them both emotionally and realistically. There will be blood glucose (sugar) fluctuations because, come on, we are playing artificial pancreas externally, after all. There is NO perfect science to this! When everything from emotions, to weather, diet, exercise, and hormones affect blood sugar, you have to understand, there is no cure for this yet for a reason: it is VERY complicated to understand and there are A LOT of variables.

Once we overcame the fact that we had to check Wyatt's blood sugar with a needle prick to his finger EVERY time he wanted to eat, felt high or low, in the middle of the night…well, pretty much every three hours, we started to adjust. We thought if we could keep him in good blood sugar range so his organs wouldn't be severely damaged, we might start feeling like we could handle things like work and outings again.

We took Wyatt to photography sessions and also trained family to watch him for longer jobs like weddings. That usually meant we tried to get him as stable as possible, then packed food that had little to no carbohydrates in it like dill pickles, cheese, and meat so that he wouldn't need an insulin shot while we were gone. It also meant we had packaged juice, in case his blood sugar went low and trained people on the signs to watch for. These low signs included: him falling down, acting weepy or crying unusually, not listening, getting angry, and then taught them to check his blood sugar. If it was below 80, they were to give him a 15 carb juice to bring his blood sugar up, then to wait 15 minutes and check him again. If he was still low, they had to repeat this process, if not, he could have a snack (his meat, cheese, or dill pickles). Wyatt liked calling those "free snacks" because if they didn't have carbohydrates in them, it meant he could have them without a shot.

One time, I remember getting ready to go to a photography session and although I had already checked Wyatt once, I just wanted to check him again. He very assertively told me, "Come on Mom! One prick at a time is enough!" My parents thought that was hilarious and he seemed empowered letting me know that he'd had enough and I needed to trust that Grandma and Grandpa had him and he was going to be just fine! Sometimes in life, we know when we have had enough and we want to just be left alone. I knew my son needed to be heard in that moment, so I respected his wishes and trusted that we had trained my parents well and they would take good care of him. He was absolutely right!

#Lesson 7: Knowing your limits:

Reflection Opportunity:

Have you ever had a time when someone or something was taking up too much of your time and you just needed to take back control? I am reminded of that by my son's outburst. We have to have balance in our lives. We need to know when we need to be in charge of some things and know when it's okay to delegate things to others. Take a few minutes to reflect and journal that experience in a notebook or share it on my Facebook author page: Trina Licavoli Gunzel.

Chapter 8
Intense Hospital-ity

This chapter is a really challenging chapter for me to write, but I feel that I have to in order to give parents information about things that are in their control. It is so frustrating when you go through something that makes you have to absolutely depend on going to the hospital and on having routine doctor's appointments and prescription refills.

My husband is an Eagle Scout and always prided himself on the fact that he could take care of us and provide for us WHEREVER we lived. We chose a home in a rural location because we liked being close to nature and not living in very populated area. Our son being diagnosed with Type 1 Diabetes changed all of that.

Now, we are dependent on insulin, doctor's appointments in order to get them refilled, and even climate makes a difference for his health. If you are reading this and work in the medical profession, thank you for taking the time to learn more! I really appreciate every one of you who truly takes the time to share your love and concern for your patients! We have had wonderful doctors and some rough medical staff everywhere we have lived. Patients, it is your responsibility to be kind and responsible with your care and take care of yourself, so keep that in mind reading this, as well.

Part of our time in the hospital included some very specific experiences that I need to share in order to pay some painful knowledge forward. I hope by sharing it will save some of the hurt for future children and parents diagnosed.

Initially, we were taken by ambulance to the Pediatric ICU part of a large hospital for care. Now, especially if there is an endocrinology department, they are used to having Type 1 Diabetics in and out, frequently. I think part of what happens in these facilities is they get desensitized to how traumatic it is for the families. I can't tell you how many times during this experience I have had to remind people, "Look, you might see this a hundred times a day, but this is our FIRST time. Please show some empathy and compassion."

We didn't really understand the whole process of what was being done to our son. The first I.V.'s that were put in him, he really didn't feel because he was in a diabetic induced coma. However, as he started to come out of it from the slow drips of insulin doses; he wanted to understand what was happening. Our son has always been a very articulate child and insisted that something was burning his toe. The nurse assured him over and over there was nothing that could be burning him. However, the monitor they had clipped onto his big toe, after pulling it off, was actually burning a hole through his toenail.

TIP #1 for caregivers: Always listen to your patient, no matter how young they are. They know their body. If they say something hurts, it probably does.

Another issue that happened was when he wanted to eat and they were ready to transition him from the IV to shots. There was not much explanation given about how this was going to happen. This is what our experience was: A meal he was excited about was promised to him, the food came, then he was told in order to eat it, he had to get a shot in the stomach. Of course he started crying and I remember the nurses holding him down and inserting a syringe of insulin into his stomach. This really didn't help him to NOT be afraid of needles, nor did it set him up for the rest of his life having a positive attitude toward getting shots for food.

TIP #2 for caregivers: Explain, model, and explain some more. There is a Rufus bear given to kids once they make it to the NEXT level and LOTS of information. While sweet, this should be giving in the I.C.U. so parents can read and understand what is going on during their day of transition. Rufus the bear and the book could help make this transition easier because having information makes things less scary. Parents should also be able to explain to their child what is going to happen, since they know their child best, to limit fear and anxiety. Again, the "push them through model" does not set them up for success for the rest of their life. Now, in all fairness, maybe we just had a bad experience, but we shared our feedback and never received any information, so this is a global way to help others on a larger scale. Hopefully parents, doctors, nurses, and anyone else interested will be able to read this in digital download format immediately and make this whole process better for everyone, TODAY!

Once we "made it through" the I.C.U., we were first put in a room shared with a child with an airborne infectious disease and told we all had to wear masks in and out of the room. We were told we had to be in that room because our child had a runny nose. I asked them to test to see what kind of infection they thought he had because my son wasn't sick. He had a runny nose because he was crying from being giving his first insulin shot in the stomach and it cleared up as soon as we blew his nose and wiped his tears. Very haughtily and huffily, we were transferred to another room with another patient and never received the swab test results indicating anything was wrong with our son, other than Type 1 Diabetes.

The next room transfer had us side by side, with just a curtain separating us, with a baby that was left alone crying almost the entire time we remained there over the next four days. Hardly anyone ever came to visit the child and after thinking I was going to lose my mind from my own grief, anxiety and screaming neighbor, I found I could only soothe him by putting my hand on the curtain where he would touch mine and seemed comforted by some company. Wyatt and I would try to sing to him to get him to sleep and sometimes a nurse would come if we really begged, but it was not a very warm welcome to the world of Type 1 Diabetes.

After waking up from little sleep sharing the hospital bed with my son, we were told we needed to order breakfast. As a new parent trying to learn how to care for my child and feed him all over again at the age of four, we were told to pick anything he wanted from the menu. We were supposed to call and order the food, and then they would teach us how to calculate the carbohydrates for him. So, Wyatt wanted orange juice, cereal, sausage, and fruit. We ordered the meal and waited, reading through some of the bags of training materials.

When the training nurse came who was supposed to teach us how to calculate his food choices and oversee us giving him his first insulin shot ourselves, she absolutely reamed us out for picking orange juice for him. I reminded her she said we could have anything off the menu and she snapped back saying that he couldn't have orange juice and I should've know that. After a frustrating first shot and everyone in tears again, she left shaking her head.

I remember talking to my husband and looking over seeing a big sign that said if we had any problems with our experience to call the hospital administrator. I had completely had enough. We were trying our best with the overwhelming new that was coming our way and I was not feeling like our costly "experience" was anything that resembled supportive or helpful. The administrator was shocked that his trainer would have acted that way and reassured me she was one of their best. I reassured him that I was a teacher and trainer too, and if that was her best, then she was failing us and the hospital.

She came back later with a new attitude and apologized to us. It seemed like it reminded her to see every patient as new again and be empathetic to their situation. Sometimes it takes experiences like that for people to wake up their emotional and empathetic side again. I have many nursing friends and can share 10 great nurse stories for every bad one, but I share this as a reminder to any who have lost their empathy after too many negative interactions and to empower Type 1 Families to make sure your voice and your unique situation and family is heard.

Get the training and information you need while you are there and take the steps to make sure you are treated fairly and kindly. You will need all of the information you can get when you take your child home and implement it continuously. Take advantage of your training stay and leave prepared, confident, and supported. We were so grateful to all of our family and friends who reached out to us with prayers, love, and support during this time. It really made a difference to have that extra boost of positivity amidst all the new and uncomfortable news. Sometimes when you don't know what to do, just showing love and kindness is the best thing you can do.

#Lesson 8: You are your own best advocate:

Reflection Opportunity:

There are so many times you want to know the reason for something or you want the medical staff to be able to tell you exactly what to do. However, in the end, it is up to you. Only you know your unique situation best. There will be times that you will need to research things, figure out and think about your best options, and share that information with medical staff that is trying to help you. Be polite, be courteous, be kind, and make sure that your needs are met. If you shut down or leave and don't get the training, medicine, or care you need because you are offended, you are only hurting yourself.

Everyone has bad days so remember to be kind and allow for humanness on both sides of the table.

Can you think about a time that you could have handled yourself better or been more prepared when you were in a situation where you needed medical attention? How would you handle the situation differently in the future? Take a few minutes to reflect and journal that experience in a notebook or share it on my Facebook author page: Trina Licavoli Gunzel.

Chapter 9

Second "First Experiences"

If you are living the life of a Type 1 child, are a Type 1 family, or know and love someone who is, you can think of this section of second "first experiences" similar to the experience of bringing home a newborn baby. EVERYTHING you normally did easily now takes at least twice as long and seems like you have to learn over from scratch. Thankfully, for us, after years of practice, we only occasionally leave our son's medical bag at home or out somewhere and have to go back. But, initially, the transition from the hospital and back into mainstream activities, for us at least, was brutal and painful.

Imagine, you leave the hospital, head overloaded with information, heart overwhelmed with emotion, arms overloaded with bags of paperwork and a training manual, and sure enough, it's time for your child to eat before you can commute the two hours home. For many, this involves a quick swing through their favorite fast food and boom; you're on your way, right? When we left, we spent the first night out of the hospital at a nearby hotel because all of our son's necessary medical supplies could not be filled until the next day. When my husband did finally get the supplies, he was scoffed at saying, "Oh man, you have the BIG bag of prescriptions." Also, he was told there weren't any of the smaller syringes available, so our son got to have the large, scary, painful needles until we could get them filled at another pharmacy. That was not a fun two days looking back. We were definitely in survive, not thrive mode at that point.

So, we were checked into a hotel, our son wanted to eat, and we were trying to learn how to feed him all over again. We decided to try a nearby chicken burrito place that seemed to have half way healthy options. I think it took us twenty minutes to make a selection we felt we could figure out the carbohydrate count for, another twenty minutes to give our son the proper insulin dose, ten minutes of answering questions from nearby people feeling sorry for us and horrified to see us pull out a needle and inject our child, and five minutes to calm down Wyatt from the shot and get him to actually eat something. Hmmmmm, there was nothing "fast" about this fast food experience for the first time, at all!

I remember thinking food wasn't fun or something we would ever enjoy again. And, I'm

Italian so many of my food memories were all about family, celebrations, and sharing recipes. This was a whole new level of first frustration I really didn't ever want to experience. It didn't seem realistic. I couldn't grasp that this was our new life.

Somehow, we managed through that day, ordered something from room service we could calculate carbohydrates close enough from the carb book we were given, and all passed out. I remember thinking about how sad I was for my little boy, how I would never wish this for him, and how there was absolutely nothing I could do about it. For the second time in my son's life, I felt like I had taken him out of the hospital as a newborn, was having to learn to feed him all over again, and would be on every three hour finger poke checks to make sure he was safe until a cure was found. This seemed impossible, for the second first time.

Praying…I prayed a lot. I always thought I prayed, but it seemed like being in constant prayer was my only saving grace and path to sanity. I learned, like I had when he was a baby, to anticipate him being hungry and have some calculated bagged snacks ready so he wouldn't have to wait, we could do a finger poke, and give him the necessary insulin more quickly. These small successes started to build until we began to put together some form of a life again. At this point, for us, our second firsts looked like this:

Then: Baby monitor

Now: Blood glucose monitor

Then: Baby formula or breast milk

Now: Juice or milk for low blood sugar

Then: Baby cried when needing something

Now: Our four year old cried from shots

Then: Baby needed to be burped and rocked

Now: Our son needed to be comforted and encouraged

Then: Grandma and Grandpa could watch our baby so we could have a date night

Now: Everyone was terrified to watch him and needed special training

Then: We could stay up all night processing photos and working

Now: We had no extra time or energy because we were staying up all night checking blood sugars

Then: Anything seemed possible

Now: Nothing seemed possible

Then: Our son loved food and to play and swim

Now: Our son tried to avoid food to avoid shots and had to be monitored closely with exercise

Then: We carried a diaper bag everywhere

Now: We carried a medical "go bag" everywhere

I could go on and on, but the big idea here is that the needs are tremendous, there is a lot of intense training and no matter what, there will be high and low blood sugar fluctuations based on diet, exercise, emotions, the weather, hormones, growth periods, excitement, sickness, and more. Everything feels like a new first. Be kind to yourself. It is a steep learning curve, even for overachievers.

I have to end this chapter on a lighter side because obviously, we are still here and are now THRIVING seven years later. For all those recently diagnosed, I promise, it will get better. I know it does NOT feel like that now, but you are not alone and your child will learn, grow, and is amazingly strong, smart, and courageous. For all those wanting to be a support to a loved one or friend with Type 1, love them, listen to them, and have them teach you all about it so you can be there for them. For all those just interested in learning about Type 1 Diabetes, bless you and your compassionate hearts for caring and sharing this information. I hope as a face is put to Type 1 and these precious family stories come out; it will inspire a cure, today, for all those long suffering, patient, people. Thank you.

#Lesson 9: What to expect when you are expecting, a cure:

Reflection Opportunity:

There will be a lifetime for you that can pass by while you wait for a cure. Don't miss it. Embrace every first moment, every first experience, every first opportunity, today! Life doesn't wait for you. Do the best you can with the information and facts you have and be true to yourself. Your body knows what you need, listen to it. Give yourself plenty of rest, laughter, and eat healthy and exercise. Save the sugar for lows and treat yourself. Most of all: love yourself and embrace your personal journey.

There is a larger purpose for your pain and only YOU can truly walk in YOUR shoes. Share your story. Make a plan for self improvement and make some promises to your better self. Take a few minutes to reflect and journal those thoughts in a notebook or share them on my Facebook author page: Trina Licavoli Gunzel.

Chapter 10

Facts And Fiction of Type 1 Diabetes

Facts:

Here's the simple breakdown of what happens when a person is told they are diagnosed with Type 1 Diabetes:

The person may or may not have been feeling badly.

The person may or may not have been losing weight.

The person may or may not have started wetting the bed.

The person may or may not have wanted to eat.

The person may or may not have been constipated.

The person may or may not have been getting misdiagnosed for months.

The person may or may not have gone into a diabetic coma prior to diagnosis.

Are you getting the picture that the diagnosis varies? We are, too.

Broken down facts (The NON TEXTBOOK VERSION):

Type 1 Diabetics have lost the ability to have their body convert food to energy because a part of their pancreas stopped working. Basically, their immune system started to recognize cells they need, as foreign bodies, and attacked them. Without those cells, they are not able to produce insulin anymore, so they must have insulin given to them through an injection (either by shots or through a pump site). The insulin helps food be absorbed and be used for energy. If they get too much insulin and/or too much exercise, they will have low blood sugar. If they do not get enough insulin, their blood sugar will go high. High and low blood sugars cause damage to the body and it is a challenge to manage blood sugar levels playing external pancreas with insulin doses. It is a very complicated autoimmune disease and while Type 1 Diabetics can look healthy, they can be having severe internal organ damage.

Dispelling Type 1 Fiction/Absurd Ideas: Please read to understand and stop these misconceptions. It can be very frustrating and disheartening to constantly re-explain these ideas:

Type 1 people did NOT get Type 1 Diabetes from eating too much candy.

Type 1 Diabetics did not do anything that caused them to get it.

There is no magic drink that cures Type 1 Diabetes, I wish there was, but there is NOT.

Type 1 Diabetes cannot be reversed with diet and exercise. (Healthy diet and exercise IS great for everyone, not just Type 1 Diabetics).

There are so many myths and stories about Type 1 Diabetes and the causes I have lost count. I have also lost track of how many times I have been given a suggestion or asked about the cause of my son's Type 1 Diabetes. These are the FACTS I know.

My husband, daughter, and I have all been tested through studies and none of us have been identified as having the gene that would cause our son to have Type 1 Diabetes. It shows he shouldn't have it, but he does so there you go. He was a healthy little boy with some occasional illnesses prior to being diagnosed. Our son enjoyed eating all types of foods, went to pre-school, and enjoyed fresh fruits and vegetables. Prior to getting diagnosed, these are the things we noticed so if this can help someone else identify Type 1 Diabetes early and save your child, we are happy to share:

Pre-Diagnoses:

Occasionally he was sick.

He did end up getting pneumonia in the spring and had an inhaler for a short period.

He had several rashes that seemed to move around his body and he would look pale and the rash was similar to hives.

He would sometimes pee and there would be frothy bubbles, like he drank bubble bath or something.

He went from wanting to eat to not wanting food.

He was always thirsty.

He couldn't hold it and seemed like he was getting bladder infections.

He occasionally wet the bed after having been potty trained for years.

He was constipated (probably from the dehydration).

Blood sugar tests came back showing he was not Type 1 Diabetic or the results were inconclusive.

Right when he was diagnosed, he was passing out and seemed like he had a cold with heavy breathing.

Our doctor was amazing and followed our case for nine months suspecting something but nothing showed that our boy was a Type 1 Diabetic until the day his blood sugar tested over 900. Luckily, we took him in immediately and still have our son, today.

Be persistent and trust your gut instincts. If you know something is wrong with your child, don't give up until you find out what it is so you can give them the best chance at a healthy full life.

Get all of the information you can get so that when you take your child home, you can implement what you have learned, continuously.

#Lesson 10: Know yourself and your kid(s):

Reflection Opportunity:

Does your child have any of the symptoms of Type 1 Diabetes? A simple blood test is an easy check and can prevent severe internal damage and even the loss of your child. I pray that families will take this information seriously and that doctors and other medical staff will use it to gain insight from personal experience and be empathetic to the real 24-7 walk with Type 1 families.

If there is someone you know who would benefit from this information, please take the opportunity to reflect and journal their information in a notebook or share this book with them and my Facebook author page: Trina Licavoli Gunzel.

Chapter 11

How To Love Your Type 1 Friends And Family

This is a really interesting chapter because you would think love just comes naturally, but there is a tendency for some people to want to be cruel when someone has something that is broken or just a little bit different. I'm not sure exactly what that comes from. Maybe it is an inherent survival of the fittest mentality or whatever, but to me it just breaks down to the simplest and best advice ever given which was to" *love one another*."

My son is not broken. He is one of the strongest people I know. I mean, come on, it takes courage to inject yourself with thousands of needles, endure painful site changes, and wear out your fingers and body with scar tissue to survive and just do the basic skill most people take for granted: eat. However, some people use this opportunity to make others feel bad or like they are "less than" just because they might not choose to eat the same things or they actually might and they just dose extra insulin for it.

There are many different Type 1 Diabetes life, diet, exercise, and schedules that people will choose to make. The biggest thing I have learned is to respect that. There are many life choices that people everywhere make that I might not necessarily make for myself, but I can choose to love them and respect them and their decision.

I wanted to make a point to share this because anyone who has been diagnosed personally, is raising, or who has raised a child with Type 1 Diabetes I am sure can give you lists of things people have told them are the reasons they or their child has Type 1 Diabetes and also a list of cures that can "fix" them. I really wish there was, but there is no "cure" I have found yet. We have found that we don't have to give our son as much insulin with certain food choices, but it's not just as simple as diet. Exercise, illness, excitement, stress, mood, and even the weather also affect blood sugar levels so the best advice I can give you on "How to love your Type 1 Friends and Family" is just this: *Love them. Listen to them.*

If you really want to help, see if you can *learn from them* how to take care of their child so they can have a date night once in a while or to help put their mind at ease in case they need help in an emergency. Sometimes it helps to hear examples of stories of how people have helped and so I want to share some of our experiences with you.

I never really understood the concept of "it takes a village to raise a child" until our son was diagnosed. I am sure most parents who have had something health wise happen to a child can relate to this, if they are in a loving community. Emotionally, physically, financially, and even spiritually, you are really tested when something like this happens. I was not used to functioning on no sleep, ever, and the constant crying of my normally happy little boy was about enough to make us all cry on a daily basis. I could no longer simply feed him or have someone help watch him so I could work and that complicated our life quickly. The added expenses for routine doctor visits, insulin, and supplies were also outrageous.

Our hometown community has always been amazing at supporting each other and I had helped at numerous benefits and fundraisers over the years for many of my friends. My heart was overwhelmed when I received a call from a friend who had a local foundation to help families that had a health crisis with their child. They reached out to us and contributed to our son's expenses and wanted to see how they could help. We also had people donate when our son was in studies for clinical trials in California for two years and we needed to help get him there and transition him from shots to a pump.

Although we were hurting, I think it is through those darkest times we are called to really reach out and speak light and love to others.

We had so many friends, family, and acquaintances that heard our story and donated to help Wyatt and it made the difference in him getting access to better studies, care, and better equipment. My husband and I are both hard working, able people who pride ourselves on our ability to help others and ourselves and it was humbling to have so many people step up and want to help us when we really needed it. We will forever be grateful.

Of course there were some who were cruel and not understanding during this time, but I can only hope that their eyes will be opened if they ever have to experience any kind of a drastic life shift due to health issues. It is truly not a path I would have chosen and I have had to do a lot of growing through this journey, but I think it has allowed me to learn a lot of lessons that I would not have otherwise known. Here are some of the things I have learned through this journey of love.

When I feel I am strong enough, I can always be stronger.

When I feel I don't understand something, there are resources to learn.

When I feel afraid, knowledge and experience is a way to overcome.

When I need inspiration and an example of the greatest love, my Bible is my greatest strength.

When I thought I was tired, I wasn't even close.

When I thought I could do anything, God humbled me to make me see I was not in control.

When I thought I had seen generosity, I saw how much more generous people could be.

When I thought I had already experienced the greatest love, I saw new depths grow.

When I thought I already loved my children, I saw how much more I could love them.

When I thought there was no hope, I found healing and comfort in the journey.

When I blamed myself for my son's diagnosis, I found that grief only heals in time.

When I thought I couldn't do something, I found that God makes all things possible.

There have been so many countless acts of love we have been overwhelmingly blessed with, I just want to say thank you. Thank you to everyone who has prayed for our family, contributed toward helping Wyatt, shared our story, encouraged someone else because of what we have been through, paid forward a generosity that was shared with you, and/or who has broadened their awareness of Type 1 Diabetes. I feel like there is a bigger reason for us going through struggles and I hope that people will feel connected and inspired to reach out to others by reading this. Thank you for thinking of others, in all situations and personal walks they are going through in their life journey, and for simply showing love to them. Health struggles can be one of the most isolating times, yet it seems like we are always connected if we will only open the doors of our hearts and receive it.

Live, laugh, and above all…love.

Invite people to parties…let them eat cake…don't be afraid…enjoy the amazing people placed in your life because of your personal journey…and grow from it.

#Lesson 11: Pay the love forward:

Reflection Opportunity:

Think about a time in your life that someone reached out and showed love to you. Maybe it was an act of kindness like bringing you a meal or helping you with a project when you didn't even ask. Has someone ever donated to a cause that you organized? Take some time to write down a specific memory and what that meant to you in your life.

Think about how you can pay that love act forward and be a blessing to someone else. Is there someone on your heart right now that you know is struggling? How can you be a source of love and light in their life? Consider taking the time to write a thank you note to someone and let them know how that gift of generosity helped you. As you reflect on those experiences, write them in a notebook or share them on my Facebook author page: Trina Licavoli Gunzel. Inspiring positivity and spreading love is wonderfully contagious!

Chapter 12

Type 1 Hero Stories

Coast to coast, we have made amazing friendships and met remarkable people who live with Type 1 Diabetes, every day. I want to dedicate this section to those specific individuals who live, breath, sleep and go to bed each night hoping to wake up to answered prayers for a cure. These are a combination of elements of their stories, with names and details changed to protect their identity.

A hero by definition is a person who is admired or idealized for courage, outstanding achievements, or noble qualities. It takes a lot of courage and dedication to be able to inject yourself, make accurate calculations, and do the hard work it takes to survive and give yourself the best chance you can at a healthy life through smart choices. Type 1 people are judged, ridiculed, and oftentimes misunderstood, but many rise to be health educators, commit to helping in studies to advance technology to work toward a cure, and are some of the strongest people I have ever met. I hope you enjoy meeting some of my favorite Type 1 Heroes I have met along the way. To all of you out there who have untold stories, I hope you feel connected, cared for, and loved as we try to spread awareness of the Type 1, 24-7 reality.

Meet My Wyatt:

Age 11

Diagnosed when he was 4

Since he can remember, Wyatt has always dreamed of being an air force pilot. It broke his heart when he learned that his diagnosis won't allow him to do that. We are hoping by expanding his interests to other fields, he will be open to other opportunities. He has a personality that is absolutely magnetic. When I say that, I mean he makes friends wherever he goes and he has a warm personality that is not easily forgotten.

Since he was diagnosed, he has been sharing about finger pokes, insulin, site changes, and carb counting with anyone who will listen. One of my favorite memories was when we were at a baseball outdoor photo session and the kids who had seen him growing up with us over the years were sitting near him. We were finishing up the individual pictures and the boys were gathering for the group picture. There was little Wyatt, sitting right in the middle of them all and he said, "Hey guys, do you want to learn about Type 1 Diabetes? I'm going to teach you all about it!" Right there, all of the JV and Varsity baseball players who were seated and standing all around him listened and learned as he explained the highs and lows of Type 1 Diabetes. From finger pokes and shots to meal ideas, those boys got a quality education from a little guy that made them all feel like they could be just a little bit tougher with anything they were faced with in life.

Lots of high fives and smiles were shared and I remember one young man telling him he was a pretty cool little kid. To me, that's a Type 1 hero at work. (My son, my little hero, sharing, educating, and putting a pretty cool face to Type 1 Diabetes.) We'll educate this world and get a cure, one team at a time. Who knows what he'll be, a farmer, a doctor, a performer, a writer? I just want him to be healthy and happy.

Meet Tiffany:

Age: 15

Diagnosed when she was born.

Tiffany was adopted by a very loving family and was diagnosed in the hospital as having Type 1 Diabetes. Tiffany has never known any different life. She has always needed insulin injections in order to process food. Without it, she would not be able to grow or live. As soon as a pump was available, she was transitioned from insulin shots to a pump. Tiffany is fearless! She competes in extreme sports and wears her pump out for all to see. She loves answering questions about it and many people think it's just an iPod. One day, she hopes to get a low dog that will go with her everywhere.

Tiffany is starting to struggle with keeping her blood sugar stable because of her changing hormones and sports schedule. She really has to make sure she has enough carbohydrates and a blood glucose level of around 120 to keep her stable overnight. Tiffany's mother is an amazing care giver and checks her every night at midnight to make sure she is safe. Her scariest moment was when a site came out while Tiffany was at camp and she had no idea how long it had been out or how much insulin she hadn't received. Those events make managing Type 1 extra challenging, but Tiffany was built strong to handle anything Type 1 Diabetes throws her way. Her courage and determination to show that Type 1 won't keep her from doing anything is inspiring!

Meet Cole:

Age: 17

Diagnosed when he was: 5

Cole wasn't showing any symptoms at all when his family took him in for his routine doctor's appointment. He had always been a fairly skinny child and was very active. It was a shock when his blood work came back that he was over 1,000 (80-

120 is a really good range for Type 1 Diabetics). His stay in the hospital was fairly uneventful. His parents got the training and worked hard to teach him and train him up as a confident, healthy, Type 1 Diabetic. His little sisters even knew how to help take care of him and would look out for him and bring him juice if they were out playing and he went low (below 80). Today, he is in high school and plays first string on the football team. He uses the high adrenalin rush to keep him in the game and doesn't wear his pump while he's playing so it won't get broken.

After years of managing this, Cole knows he will have to be up checking his sugar to catch the low blood sugar at night that inevitably comes after that much excitement and adrenalin. He is blessed with a very supportive and encouraging family who takes great care of him and looks out for him. It is still physically and mentally exhausting for them all, but they have learned how to manage it and continue on with their lives using all the technical advancements that exist. With so many apps, device sharing, and pump technologies, they feel they have a pretty good knowledge of Type 1 and it doesn't hold them back.

Meet: Ricky

Age 5

Diagnosed when he was 5

Ricky was just diagnosed the summer before he

started Kindergarten. Both of his parents work full time and are divorced. Ricky has to share time between them, trading every other weekend. Because of his parents not being able to get on the same page about Ricky's treatment and insulin management program, Ricky's doctor has chosen to have them on a set carbohydrate schedule with an old fashioned style of insulin dosing. They only use shots, no pump. Ricky has to have one shot during the day to cover his carbohydrate count for the day, and one shot at night to cover his long term acting insulin.

Ricky's dad takes him to kindergarten on the first day, tells the school his child has Type 1 Diabetes, hands them his blood glucose meter and leaves. He tells them he has a soda in his backpack in case he goes low. The school is left to determine how to take care of the child and what needs to be done. Ricky is pale and passes out on the playground because his blood sugar goes too low during recess. This is going to be a very challenging life for Ricky if he cannot get some support and training. The school works with the parents to set up a 504 Plan so they can meet his needs at school and help understand his treatment better.

High and low blood sugars have an effect on brain development, growth, internal organ damage, and later result in loss of limbs, blindness, and can even cause death. It is intense to manage and the school is concerned about this child's health and safety. After six months in the present school district, Ricky moves. The parents say they need to be closer to better doctors to help manage his care.

Meet: Connie

Age 17

Diagnosed – Never officially

Connie was always a super skinny kid. She loved to play sports and there was no history of any form of diabetes in her family. It was embarrassing for her to tell her mother that she had been wetting the bed, but she knew something was wrong. Her parents drove her to the emergency room. They suspected diabetes but her results showed only borderline results. She was told to go home and keep monitoring it and come back if there were any changes.

Several weeks later, Connie was playing in a volleyball game and just didn't feel right. She needed to stop and drank a juice she had thrown in, just in case she felt low. When she checked her blood sugar, she was only 54. That night, Connie was tired so she just went to sleep. She didn't want to wake her parents after returning late home from her game. In the middle of the night, Connie's blood sugar went too low. She was tired and didn't wake up to check her blood sugar. There was nobody to wake her up and help her and she tragically died in her sleep. Her brokenhearted parents found her unresponsive in the morning. Her story must be shared so that others can be saved.

Meet: Talon

Age 14

Diagnosed when she was 8

Talon is having a rough time in Jr. High. Having Type 1 Diabetes wasn't a big deal when he was in elementary school, but teenagers were different. After having his pump site ripped out by some bullies, not being allowed to go to the nurse to get his low snacks when he had severely low blood sugar by a substitute teacher, being questioned about his glucagon gun, monitor, supplies, and issues about where he was allowed to check his blood sugar, his family made the decision to switch to homeschooling for this period of his life. Later, Talon went back to high school and graduated. He said he was so happy they made that decision because high school kids all had their own groups and it didn't matter that he had Type 1 Diabetes. Actually, many kids thought it was cool. Jr. High was a rough stage of his life managing all the highs and lows of his blood sugar and hormones anyway, so he encourages other people not to be afraid to make changes and try new things.

Meet: Davin

Age 32

Diagnosed when he was 16

Davin's parents were getting divorced when he was diagnosed so he was really on his own with his management. He was very active with sports and used insulin shots and diet management the best he could. That usually meant scrounging an apple or some leftover pizza at home and grabbing a candy bar and a soda at lunch. Davin had frequent highs and lows and ended up in the hospital in DKA several times a year. However, as Davin matured and got out on his own, he started to really get really tight control of his blood sugar.

Eventually, he met someone he loved and they were still able to have children. His wife is a great help and support to him and so far, neither of their kids has been diagnosed. Davin hopes that his health will continue to be strong, so he is able to provide for his family and continue working. He knows that high and low blood sugars are just a part of his everyday life, and he must be aware of them and be prepared to treat them so that he can be safe doing things like driving, operating equipment, and he sets alarms at night to wake him after extreme exercise.

I hope meeting some of these Type 1 Heroes will add faces to the need for a cure. Every day, the struggle is real, the effort is constant and only the most courageous and diligent can survive. If you would like to share your story, please contact me or post it on my Facebook page: Trina Licavoli Gunzel.

#Lesson 12: Every day heroes:

Reflection Opportunity:

Do you know any courageous or outstanding individuals who do amazing things to survive? I can think of many who come to mind including those who battle with cancer, undiagnosed illnesses, Type 1 Diabetes, severe depression, and other life threatening conditions. So many people fight quiet battles every day and I want them to know they are not forgotten. A cure may not exist yet, but their every day struggle for survival is real. I hope this encourages your heart and you feel connected, knowing you are not alone.

The present day cure is love and we can do that for one another. Please think about someone you might be able to reach out to. Your efforts could help them go from surviving their battle to thriving and overcoming it. Won't you join me in this shout out to those who need to know they are not alone? Post your love for them on my wall in an effort of encouragement. #LOVE on my Facebook author page: Trina Licavoli Gunzel.

Chapter 13

What's Worked For Wyatt:

Sharing tips, tricks, diet, and schedule from our Type 1 life and hearts to yours

There are so many things we have learned after seven years of living as a Type 1 family and it seems like we continue to learn more every day. The phases of living with this autoimmune disease are more complex than I ever dreamed. I know there are some that put on a face that everything is great and try to display that it doesn't affect them, and maybe for them that is true, but that has not been our reality. I feel like it's important to share that because the overwhelming amount of people who live with this every day have had it impact their lives, greatly. Obviously for the person managing it on a daily basis, even if they are doing "great," it still takes a tremendous effort to be achieving "great" results. It takes constant 24-7 management and then there are still fluctuations in blood sugar due to weather, stress, sickness, excitement, hormones, etc. Welcome to our world! Our life no longer easily fits in a 9-5 box.

My family has went through each phase of recovery through this experience including just barely surviving living daily as a Type 1 Family to #THRIVING. It has not always been pretty, but we have been consistently making progress, so there's hope for you! As you are reading this information, of course, you need to apply whatever works best for your unique situation. Some people have diet restrictions or allergies that won't allow them to eat certain things or find that certain products work best for them, by all means, do what works for you! I am not a doctor, but I have far more hands on 24-7 real life application experience than anyone who doesn't actually have it or care for someone living with it night and day. With that, I want to share some tips, tricks, diet, and schedule from our Type 1 life and hearts to yours.

TIPS

Tip #1, being in studies helped all of our family learn some intense, in depth training, and information that you just can't seem to find anywhere else. We will forever be grateful for the staff members and training through studies we received at Stanford in California. It really changed our life and if you get the opportunity to participate in studies to help advance learning about and technology for Type 1 Diabetes, there are tremendous benefits. Our ultimate goal is for a cure, but there are many advances in technology that have helped those living in the NOW with Type 1, every day. So there's tip #1, participate in studies, when and if you can.

Tip #2, check with the airlines to see if they will help sponsor any medical studies with the hospital you are working with. We actually helped setup a sponsor program with Southwest and Stanford that made flights free for our son and one parent while he was in part of a study. There is also a program called Angel Flights we learned about that has criteria for distance and times, but they volunteer flight services as well. It takes some effort, but it really helps to offset the expenses if you need treatment for a life threatening condition or to participate in some studies. You might get a no, but you might be able to do the work to get a yes. Think outside the box and do the hard work necessary.

Tip #3, when flying with your Type 1 Diabetic supplies, we have found that taking insulin pens works well because then we don't have to refrigerate the NovoLog, as long as we carry it with us and keep it below 80 degrees. Our son is on a pump now, but even when we were using two types of insulin for shots, we found we were able to just draw out of the pen syringes. We would just take a small baby bottle cooler pack and put an ice bag in that container with the insulin for travel.

Tip #4, always have some kind of low supplies with you. We have created a "go bag" our son takes with him everywhere. In there, we carry back up supplies in case we need to change a site, syringes and extra insulin in case his pump breaks, a carb counting book, extra bandages, batteries, a glucagon gun, and some form of low supplies. Our low supplies include liquid gel squeezable candy, juice, raisins, etc. so that no matter where we are, we aren't stuck without something for him. We travel and are outdoors a lot and in locations where supplies aren't always readily available so it is important to have that "go bag" with us at all times. We have learned this the hard way, especially when we've thought we'd just run out quickly for something. You never know when there will be a traffic jam, road closure, lock down, or emergency and you don't want to be without your life saving supplies. *Check supplies BEFORE leaving the house!

Tip#5, when we attended camp, midnight checks were mandatory. Overnight, many don't like to talk about it, but people die from having their blood sugar go too low. We have learned that especially after a day of strenuous exercise or extreme weather, our son has a tendency to go low, so we check his blood sugar in the night to avoid that from happening. For our son, we have learned that if he is about 120 on his BG when he goes to bed, as long as it was a pretty routine day, he will usually hold overnight. But, I still check him in the night to make sure. We have had times for no reason that his blood sugar will just plummet and I have checked him around 2 am and he was 54. When in doubt, get up and check, an extra finger poke could save a life, maybe yours. (Yes, I sound like your mom, I AM A MOM! If you have Type 1 Diabetes, please take care of yourself! You are loved!) Doctors, please train patients on this! We have never had a doctor even suggest this outside of attending camp or studies and it can save lives!

Tip #6, try using milk to treat low blood sugar. If you can drink it, try drinking milk instead of juice to raise your blood sugar. It won't give you the drastic spike, but will bring your blood sugar up and hold it better because of the protein and carbohydrates in it. (Our son likes about a ½ cup to a cup of milk with some chocolate syrup in it for a low "treat.") It makes him feel like there are some perks to this whole Type 1 lifestyle change.

Tip #7, save the sweets for special events out, but don't bring them in the house except for low supplies. I know this one is kind of hard to swallow, but we have found that by not bringing in outside store bought sweets, we are all doing better blood sugar wise. When our standard at home is to eat healthy, our son has stable and amazing blood sugar results. Then, when we do the occasional birthday party out or want to try a fun dessert at a restaurant, it is just an occasional high blood sugar for a short while. I know some people will freak out at this tip, but it's just something we've noticed that's worked for our family that you might consider trying. I'm at the age where the pounds just don't fly off after I've had cookies, pie, or ice cream like they used to, so when I model healthy food choices, my kids are making those choices too. We've put sugar back in its place as an occasional treat, not an everyday staple.

Tip #8, on sick days; try to have some dissolvable Zofran always on hand. We have found that when our son is vomiting and has a fever, if he is not able to keep down any liquids or medicine, things can go south really fast. Our personal goal has been to try to keep him out of the hospital and from going into DKA again. So far, we have been able to do that, but sick days are the toughest. If not Zofran, talk to your doctor about something you can have on hand so that if your child can't stop vomiting, you can work to do something to keep them hydrated.

I've also had peach juice or ginger ale recommended as something to try, if you need to give them something and they are low and sick. Of course, always follow your sick day program, call your doctor, and work through your sick day plan together. Those are intense times and I have found that writing down times, doses, and keeping track of keytones, blood glucose readings, and any food and liquid intake is really helpful as a caregiver. Especially when talking to doctors over the phone to help make decisions. Sometimes taking them into the hospital is the only way, especially when you can't get their blood sugar down or stop the vomiting, and you just have to roll with that.

Thankfully we live in a modern world with access to health care and insulin so do what you need to do to get better and take the best care of yourself you can. I am so thankful for awesome health care workers that are there when we need them! If you have any questions, take your kid in or get yourself to the hospital! Don't mess around. If you can't drive, here's a bonus tip, call 911 and go by ambulance. You get RIGHT in and are able to avoid waiting in the waiting room. The cost is between you and your insurance, but if you need a straight ticket in, I highly recommend it.

Tip #9, for all of you swimmers out there, we have found that if we can get our son to take a break every 2-3 hours, put his pump back on, and do a finger poke, we can get him some insulin or a snack, and keep him in a good range. We have also found that if we unscrew the insulin reservoir while it is off of him, then screw it back in when we put it on again, it will give him the insulin he missed while he had it off instead of just dripping it out while it's off. If you are going to do this, you NEED TO REMEMBER TO TWIST THE RESERVOIR BACK IN!

We have forgotten to do that, then wondered why he's really high, and caught that it wasn't screwed back in all the way. Obviously, if the reservoir isn't screwed in, your child won't be getting the insulin they need (or you if you're wearing the pump) so don't forget to check that. If you do, the high afterward will make you remember because that's not fun to go through. Again, that is your responsibility, just think through what makes sense.

Tip #10, continue learning. There are new advances, dietary information, and networks to help you. Don't be afraid to try to improve your health. You are worth it! Make YOU your #1! Growing our own food, moving, and participating in studies have all helped my son feel #1.

TRICKS

Now for some tricks! If you want to know some of the best tricks on the planet for anyone living with or caring for someone with Type 1 Diabetes, go to some of the Bearskin Meadow Camps! They are amazing! We learned more over the two summer camps we attended than anywhere else. There are on site doctors, trainings, and the real life, down to earth, nitty-gritty, ins and outs of Type 1 daily and nightly work, care, and functions.

The Diabetic Youth Foundation offers many wonderful programs and trainings throughout the year and is located in the Concord, California area. I really can't say enough good things about them and how attending Camp Bearskin Meadow Family Camps changed our lives, for the better! I have heard of other camps in the Pleasanton, California area and through the JDRF, but Camp Bearskin Meadow in the Sequoia National Forest is my personal favorite.

Once you have been there, you really feel like if you can survive camp, you can thrive with Type 1 Diabetes. The kids are all so proud to be there with other kids who have Type 1 Diabetes. Many of the camp counselors do, too, and it is an emotional bonding time where you really learn the ins, outs, and behind the scenes information necessary to successfully manage Type 1 Diabetes. Honestly, we were so frustrated with our care and endocrinology doctors in Arizona that we actually moved states if that tells you anything about the first two years of our life, before we attended camp in California.

We ended up deciding to move to Missouri because St. Louis Children's hospital has study options available and the cost of living was more affordable, but I love that camp options and activities in California are always an option. I haven't found any better, so please let me know if you do and email me at trina@trinagunzel.com. I am always eager to learn about new opportunities to help my son and others! Thank you!

Another trick I would like to share with you is to get involved. Especially early on, meet and network with other families that have Type 1 Diabetes. I remember feeling so lonely and lost because nobody else could really relate to what we were going through on a daily basis. I just wanted to have some people in my life who absolutely understood what I was talking about. Those early friends I made at camp, I am still friends with today, and it just helps to have that little life line of understanding out there. No matter how long it's been seen you've spoken, they just get it. So, here are some tricks I've learned to beat the loneliness that creeps in when you are a Type 1 Family:

Go to camp or training somewhere

Find some support groups for Type 1 Diabetes, online or in person

Go to some of the fun JDRF events! It makes you feel like a rock star for having Type 1!

Do a fundraising walk for the JDRF! Help raise money and awareness for Type 1, and have some fun, too! We've "done the walk," got the t-shirts, raised awareness, raised money, and helped the JDRF. We are still anxiously awaiting a cure, but there have been some awesome advances in technology that sure are making living with it NOW better!

Find some great Type 1 friends that you can brainstorm ideas with, share babysitting times with for date nights, and enjoy hanging around. Not all of these friendships will work out, and that's okay, but those that you do make are truly like the best kinds of family and will last forever!

If your child is attending public school, help do some training and get your medical 504 in place so that your child's needs will be met.

Do whatever activities you want to, but feel free to say NO, too. That is probably one of the best tricks I've learned. Just because everyone is going to an event sick, doesn't mean we have to. I would rather give up one night now, than have my family down for two weeks. Really, do the things you want to in life and save your energy for the things that really matter.

Leave some gas in the tank! My husband always says that and he is absolutely right. Inevitably, after a night you've stayed out too late, gotten run down, not been eating healthy, and are exhausted, that is when your Type 1 child will get sick and you will have to bring your best A game to take care of them. Give yourself ways to say no so that you can take care of yourself and your family. YOU all are the most important people in your life and you deserve your best. Remember, you can't help others if you haven't taken care of yourself. There is only so much of you to go around, so be good to yourself. Taking time to recharge your batteries is not being a failure. It's being a smart decision maker.

DIET

Well, here you go, in this section, I am going to tell you exactly what to eat, when, and how, and you will be cured! I wish! I'm sorry but Type 1 Diabetes doesn't work that way. We have tried some of the drinks and special diets and still been told: Well, I wouldn't try this with children. So, here are the most simple diet ideas we have come up with that have worked for us. Feel free to try them and integrate them into your life, with your necessary dietary needs.

*Try eating your protein first, it slows down the rest of the food and will keep your blood sugar from spiking.

*Eat a variety of vegetables and fruits. (Grow as many of your own whole foods as you can!)

*Drink milk, soy milk or almond milk for low blood sugar for a steady holding blood sugar.

*Use juice for low blood sugar for a quick spike.

*Eat vegetables and nuts for snacks.

*Pickles, olives, hard boiled eggs, nuts, and jerky make fun in between meal snacks (that are almost carb free!).

*Try not to bring foods with white, bleached, or enriched flour into your home.

*Try not to bring foods with sugar into your home, unless they are for low blood sugar supplies.

Doesn't this sound like trying to have a healthy diet is important? Isn't that a healthy choice for everyone? We have made this life change over throughout our cupboards and fridge in our home and it's been great for all of us. Just trying to always have a protein, a fast carb, and a slow carb on a plate and minimizing the sugar has made a drastic difference for us. If you need some form of scripted program, we have really liked the "Diet Free Life," by Robert Ferguson. There's a 7 day free trial at http://jongunzel.yourwellnessroom.com you can see.

#Lesson 13: Sometimes say YES!

Reflection Opportunity:

There are many practices, ideas about, and strategies to managing a Type 1 Diabetic Diet. We have been told certain things were not able to be tried with children because of their need for carbohydrates and a varied diet to grow. We have tried certain diets that were too restrictive and weren't sustainable for our young son. One of the best things a doctor ever told us was, if you're at a birthday party and your son wants to eat cake, let him. Try to moderate the sweets, but sometimes, it's fine. I think that word MODERATION is so applicable to so many things in life.

Can you think about a time that you would have been fine doing something if it had just been done in moderation? I know I love to eat a slice of cherry pie occasionally, and done in moderation, it doesn't hurt me. But, if I sit down and eat a whole pie daily, I am going to have major problems. Make a list of things in your life that you need to work on moderating. Write down how you can bring balance to your life in those areas by doing the right amount for YOU! If you want, share your ideas on my Facebook author page: Trina Licavoli Gunzel.

Chapter 14

The 24—7 Type 1 Life

Oftentimes, when faced with challenges, we struggle to overcome new obstacles that are presented. We seek to find some sort of balance and regain our momentum. As we come to the realization that our life will never again fit into whatever nice neat boxes we thought we'd created, we are able to redefine our life and our priorities. We can find a new schedule that accommodates our energy levels, health needs, and our new reality.

One thing we found helpful was to create a variety of schedules and keep reworking them until we found one that worked for us. I encourage you to really try to think outside the box and look at all of the things you really want to have in your life that you can't seem to make time for. Start by putting those in your schedule first. Then, put in the things you absolutely must do. When you look at really prioritizing yourself and your emotional/physical needs, it seems easier to say no to things that will try to take away your precious time that really aren't adding value to your life. We give away our time like it's free to anyone that seems to need us, yet, it is the one thing we can't get back that is the only way we can get what we need and want to, done!

I'm going to include our sample schedule because we often get company that take pictures of it. We posted it on the side of our refrigerator so we can reference it and follow it, but many others have noticed it and are inspired and encouraged by it. So be bold, be brave, and don't be afraid to create a schedule for you and your family that is designed for your personal success. Our schedule is pretty tight but we also are fee to adjust it when we need to. However, having a schedule this specific really helps us to fight for the things we really need that keep us healthy: exercise, regular meals and snacks, rest, work, and play time. I was really resistant to such a structured routine, but there is enough flexibility in there for my artsy free self to thrive!

Schedule For Success

5:30 Wake up-Start the day with Gratitude & Prayer Together

5:45 Water, Snack, Supplements

6:00 Scripture Study, Goal Setting, Diet Free

	Life / other Inspirational Video/Workout
6:30-7:30	Shower and Make Breakfast
8:00	Eat Family Breakfast
8:30-9:00	Clean up
9-11:30	Play/Work/School/Chores
10:00	Family Snack
11:30	Lunch Prep
12-12:30	Family Lunch
12:30-2:30	Nap/Focused Work Time/Reading
2:30	Family Snack/Workout Time – Cardio or Strength Training
3:30-6:00	Family Play/Work/School
4:30	Family snack
6:00	Dinner Prep
6:30	Eat Family Dinner
7:00	Kids Bedtime Prep
7:15	Story, Song, and Prayer
7:30	Kids in Bed for Tuck-ins
7:45-9:00	Couple Time

8:30 Evening Snack –NO FAST CARBS!

9:00 Lights Out!

9:30 Sleeping

Now if you look at this schedule and think, "Do they ever really pull this off?" I will tell you honestly, when our life is following this schedule, it is working like a well oiled machine. Everything feels in balance and it seems we have time for everything. My son's blood sugars are more stable, we are more fit and in shape/losing weight, and we are able to achieve the goals we set for ourselves. This also works for our home school schedule.

We run our own business from home so this allows us to have time to write, create, discuss, schedule on-line meetings, etc. If this isn't your optimum schedule, it doesn't have to be. It is the one we personally designed for us! But, feel free to use it, adjust it, and make a schedule that works for you and your life. If you want to try it out, go for it! You can always use it as a starting point and by all means, personalize it! Mine says: Gunzel Family Schedule For Success!

#Lesson 14: Don't be afraid of scheduling:

Reflection Opportunity:

I was always afraid that scheduling would take away my flexibility. I really love to "go with the flow" and do things spur of the moment. However, I have found that by working together with my husband who loves to organize and schedule, we can strike that balance. Just schedule in time for "play" or have some open blocks that are during your "flow" time so you can direct your creative energy toward projects you want to accomplish.

Take some time to write down your idea of your perfect schedule for your life. Then, see how close you can get to making your life match your desired reality. It's YOUR life! You can be in control of getting more time to do the things you really love. See if there are some things you can cut out that are just wasting your precious gift of time. Share your great ideas on my Facebook author page: Trina Licavoli Gunzel.

Chapter 15

Hope For A Cure And Have Success, TODAY

Yes, we would love to see a cure as soon as possible. Yet, we can't sit around and wait for one. We have to make the best choices for our son to have the best chance at a healthy full life, today! I hear of advances and a cure coming today, just like I did seven years ago. I have been through so many fazes of hopelessness, hopefulness, being excited, thinking the next study we were in would bring about the cure, stepping away from diabetes, embracing diabetes, and again, we are in hopeful and rally mode. I am so hopeful and prayerful for a cure, but, as a mother helping her son live with Type 1 Diabetes, today, I know that life doesn't wait.

I can't sit around waiting for a cure while our life passes by. I have tried having my son do the lemon water cleanse and the okra water and he doesn't want to live just drinking that, and he still had to have his insulin. We have to work to find a balance that works for us that also includes a quality of life TODAY. I think many people forget to include the "will to live" in the equation. I know we have worked really hard at that helping him grow from four to eleven and will continue to help and encourage him throughout his life.

One big thing I'd like you to think about is this: Find a way to win every day. If you live your life beat down by diabetes one day at a time or one meal at a time, you will be miserable. I can say that because I have been there. You have to celebrate the little victories and start building some positive momentum toward success. How is your overall quality of life? Are you happy with your A1C levels? If not, is there anything you are willing and able to do to improve them?

We went from high A1Cs and horrible care to studies, technology advances, and even moving to get our son the lowest A1C he ever had. When our doctor thought we were doing everything possible and were his Type A Superstar Family, we took it to a whole new level by overhauling our cupboards and switching our diet to a Diet Free Life Program.

There are always ways to improve, if we are willing to work to implement changes. When we find something that works, we want to embrace that and then when we get too comfortable, try to see if we can improve again. I have learned no matter how much I think I know about this, I always have more to learn and each day brings new challenges and successes, too, so find some and embrace yours, today!

#Lesson 15: Find a way to win:

Reflection Opportunity:

In case you do not have a cure today, find a way to win. If you are part of experiencing a cure today, celebrate and share that! I guarantee that even if there was a cure somewhere invented today, there isn't a way for everyone who has Type 1 Diabetes to have immediate access to it everywhere.

There have been some major advances in treatment and care over the years, but many lives have come into this world and passed through without a cure. THEY LIVED! What can you do to embrace and celebrate your life, TODAY? What awesome things are you grateful for? My family has adopted some family cheers we shout after we exercise together or complete a project together. It just makes us feel like we had a win. We actually put our hands in the middle and shout: Gunzel Family, We WIN! As we do this, we raise our arms up in the middle in just a little celebration to get a "yes!" moment in our lives.

What do you do to celebrate your wins? Write them down in your notebook and do your own personal victory dance, cheer, or pat yourself on the back to recognize and encourage yourself. You are trying and that is something to celebrate! Share your great ideas on my Facebook author page: Trina Licavoli Gunzel.

Chapter 16

Recovering And Healing From Grief: Acceptance and forgiveness

It took me seven years to forgive myself for whatever reasons I had put together to blame myself for causing my son to get Type 1 Diabetes. Of course through all the testing, nothing ever proved it was my "fault," but as a parent, I just wanted to know WHY this happened to my son. I really took it personally for a long time. Very naively, I grew up thinking if I was just a "good girl," followed the rules, was faithful and obedient to the Lord, and tried my best, bad things wouldn't happen to me or my family. My choices kept me from a lot of other trials and personal struggles, but I learned that it is very easy to have faith when things are going well, but it is through trials, when your faith is really tested, that you grow the most.

I remember when my son was diagnosed that for the first time in my life, I actually felt really angry at God. I didn't understand how or why this could happen to MY son. After all, I had followed all the rules! I had done everything I possibly could, and yet, my son still was suffering through this and there was nothing I could do to take it from him. It was through that lonely realization that I had a change of heart, almost instantly, and knew that the ONLY way I was every going to make it through this, and be all that I needed to be for my son and my family, was by the grace of God.

I had to take comfort in the tremendous love our Savior has for us and know that by his example of enormous suffering on the cross, our burden was made light. I understood that going through that experience was the only way He could ever reach us and be with us, no matter what struggle, pain, or situation we encountered on this earth. Quiet time spent in prayer and reflection prepared my heart for the road ahead as I sat by my son's bedside those many hours in the hospital.

It has been seven years now since our son was diagnosed and I have finally been able to forgive myself. I have searched and tried everything to identify the cause of this and to find a cure for my son. This process has taken me to a deeper place of grief, healing, and understanding than I ever imagined. I see now that we have had to go through this struggle in order to be able to relate to and help others. If we didn't, we wouldn't have this story to share, we wouldn't have a way to connect with every Type 1 Family that has ever lived, will be, or the family, friends, and medical professionals who care for and work with them. This knowledge and push as an author, teacher, and artist to get our message out and put a face to Type 1 Diabetes by sharing the behind the scenes reality of it, gives me strength and helps me to see a purpose for our pain.

Healing comes through many tears, seeking out wisdom, and quiet time spent in prayer. I have cried more tears than I care to count and been physically and emotionally sick over this. I don't want to be sad about it anymore. I don't want to hate myself because of it anymore. We used to have a monthly melt down session where my son would sob because he didn't want to get shots anymore and he just wanted to be able to eat and be a kid like he was before, again. Seeing him struggle and not be able to do anything about it was heartbreaking to watch. We have tried many things including art, music, snuggle and movie days, outdoor experiences, and praying as sources of emotional growth and strength. All of these things have really helped and so has just the strength that comes from living with it for so long.

When things are first so different and new, they can be overwhelming. Every poke, site change, technology change, and transition brings an element of stress and then later, strength from confidence in knowing you can do it. Personally, I know that it is my faith in God and the strength Christ gives me that allows me to do the things I need to do for my son and my family. I will honestly say that is the only way I have made it through this. I know that this entire situation and life change has been too much for us to handle alone because it IS way more than we can handle.

But, we have had such a generous outpouring of love, prayers, and support from so many friends, family, and sometimes people we don't even know, but who have heard our story, that I know this is so much bigger than us. My precious son says, "Mom, everyone has their cross to bear and having diabetes is just mine. I'm not going to let it keep me from doing anything!" He is young but he is so wise and has such a tender, strong, and courageous heart. I really do feel blessed to be his mother.

Any parent who has ever bore the guilt and tore themselves up trying to figure out what they could have done differently that would have resulted in a different outcome for their child, I have to give you this advice: If your child is still on this earth, talk to them about it. If your child is in heaven, have some time outside where you can speak aloud to them. Tell them how you are feeling and ask them for your forgiveness.

I had a real talk with my boy and I let him know that I was heartbroken that he had Type 1 Diabetes. I asked him if he would forgive me if there was something I had done that caused him to get it and if he was going to be okay. He said,

"MOM! This is NOT your fault. I'm okay Mom and you know what, I'm even glad I have Type 1 Diabetes because it has made us have a better life!" I had to own that and know that if he was okay, then I had to be okay, too. The night we had that talk, I felt like a HUGE weight lifted that I had been carrying for a long time. No matter what the reason is that my son has this, it has been a life changing event we are going to use to make us better, to make us find new ways to help others, and to show that it is possible to overcome any challenge life throws your way.

We are real with each other and talk about our feelings as a family. When our children know we hurt and see that we seek out help when we need it, they will follow that example. I always want my kids to know that they have options to overcome grief and they are never alone in what they are going through. I hope that by modeling and sharing this example, parents will take time to reach out to their kids. There are very lonely experiences and challenges we face in life and sometimes, if someone would just take the time to reach out and join us, we might overcome them better. My son felt empowered when he saw that I was struggling and needed to know that he was okay. We are not alone!

#Lesson 16: Love heals broken hearts

Reflection Opportunity:

We have all experienced times in our lives when we have been sad or upset about the outcome of something. Looking back, I have come to realize it's more about the journey. How we handle things when we are faced with impossible decisions says a lot about us. If you are facing something that is hurting your heart right now, I just want to encourage you to pray. If you are lonely, seek out comfort from your friends and family. Please don't go through your struggles alone and, if you are feeling like you are in a dangerous situation, I beg you to get the help you need.

Overcoming grief is a process and for some it takes longer than others, but be kind to yourself, know you are loved, and know there is a purpose for your pain you will be able to look back and understand someday. Take some time to write down some things you have already overcome in your life and the wisdom you have gained now that you are on the other side of the situation!

Chapter 17

Embracing The Sweet Life

I have to tell you something that most people don't ever like to talk about. We had been trying to have another child before Wyatt was diagnosed and we had a really complicated miscarriage that almost killed me.

We were so excited and waited until after about six weeks to tell people, because we'd had a miscarriage before. Honestly, we were absolutely fine just having one child, but we thought it might be nice for our son to have a sibling later in life, so we were really looking forward to it. At our almost twelve week check up, we had an ultrasound and they weren't able to find the heartbeat. Our doctor apologized and I was told I would probably have a miscarriage soon. I was hopeful, but started spotting, cramping, and a few days later, ended up going to the emergency room because the bleeding wouldn't stop.

Getting an IV. put in is never the most comfortable experience, but after 12 missed pokes, finally a sixth nurse was able to get my line in. I was examined by the ER doctor and told that I was just having a miscarriage and it was late so he didn't want to bother my doctor, who was also pregnant at the time. He gave me some pain medicine and still bleeding, I was sent home.

I really didn't feel right, but we didn't know what else to do, so my husband started driving me the forty minutes home. I kept feeling worse and worse and before we got to our street, I told him I was going to be sick and had him pull over. I threw up and just gushed out. I was covered in blood like some horror movie and sobbing for my husband to just get me home. He didn't know what to do with me so I told him to just help put me in the back of the truck. He put down the tailgate and I just laid down across it as he drove me down our street to our house.

It was about midnight and really cold outside. I sat shivering as he came out of the house with towels for me so I could take off my blood covered clothes. My father in law was staying with us watching my son and has always been there at every humiliating and crazy time in my life. This was another one of those times and he helped Jon get me into the house. I got in the shower, but the amount of blood I was losing was not normal and was more like a bright red open wound. I got out of the shower, sat on the toilet, and started to pass out. Jon was there and ended up calling 911.

Before I knew it, my house was full of people, and I was taken out on a stretcher and into an ambulance. They were unable to get another line in my arm after five more missed needle pokes. I begged them to stop trying and they let the hospital know they thought I might need a blood transfusion when I got there.

When we showed up for the second time, my doctor had been called and she was extremely upset that she hadn't been notified the first time. I was grateful to see her but remember going to sleep crying being told I had to have a D&C. When I was miscarrying, something stuck and I was hemorrhaging. If we wouldn't have gone back in for that surgery, I would've bled to death.

I never wake up very well from anesthesia and was disoriented sobbing that I'd lost the baby when I woke up. It was such an awful experience and I was so terribly sad. Miscarriages are so personal and I didn't realize how common they actually are for women until I have shared about my experience. You will always hold those hopes and dreams you had for that child in your heart. It takes a long time to heal from that loss and especially if you really wanted to have children, all of the effort, physical, and mental healing you have to do is really a process. My mother in law had the great idea to help me plant a little healing flower garden and it helped to have my hands in the soil and to do something I could do something about. Beautifying a little place that I could go out to and take care of was one of her many wonderful ideas that she shared with me to overcome grief.

It wasn't long after that I was at the hospital lying in bed with my son. I was holding him after we found out he was diagnosed with Type 1 Diabetes and our world was spinning again. I was SOOOOOOOOOOOO thankful we hadn't gotten pregnant after we'd been trying again and told my husband that I WAS DONE! I knew there was NO WAY I could do this having to care for Wyatt and everything we now had to learn. If we added a new baby to the mix, I thought I would lose my mind! So, we just decided to be grateful for our one amazing son and were going to do the best we could to take care of him with this new hurdle we'd been presented with.

After we got Wyatt home, we were working on figuring out our routine and my in-laws decided this was the year they wanted to do The Polar Express as a family. We weren't really sure we were quite ready for that, but we decided to do it so we could make that family memory. It was a wonderful trip and we found we could do more than we thought we could. Carb counting out at the restaurants was a little bit of a challenge and again, we got to deal with the horrified looks giving our son his insulin pen shot doses, but, we did it. I think we will always love The Polar Express because of that trip together. It was fun to just laugh, spend time with loved ones, and feel “normal” again. I really wasn’t feeling that great, though. For some reason I just didn’t feel like eating much and was really tired.

I thought I must have picked up something on the trip because I started throwing up the week after we got home. However, nobody else seemed to catch it. Again, I was not a napper but I just couldn’t seem to stay awake in the afternoons. Then, it hit me! Nauseous, more tired than normal, hmmmm….could I be??? NO! I went and bought a pregnancy test on the next trip we took to town and for Christmas, I gave Jon a wrapped up package with a bow on it. Inside was our pregnancy test that showed positive! We all cried and then really celebrated because although WE thought we couldn’t handle anymore, God’s plan was better!

Wyatt told us from the beginning he was going to have a baby sister. He said he had prayed for her and we didn’t need an ultrasound because he just knew we were having a girl. He was so convinced we actually did end up getting an ultra sound to find out. Sure enough, he was right!

Abbigail Rose Gunzel was our biggest surprise and greatest blessing. Our little family of three was hurting so badly emotionally. I am sure Wyatt was over smothered with all of the constant finger pokes, blood sugar checking, worry and fuss over just him. I know she complicated things, but Abbie also just made Type 1 not the only thing we did. We were tired and up in the night checking blood sugar anyway, we might as well feed and change a baby. It seems comical looking back now, but there were times I was so exhausted I just didn't think I was going to make it!

Having our children has been the best way for us to grow, learn, laugh, cry and experience this life TOGETHER. When I was younger, I never really knew if I would even want to get married or have children because I thought I might actually want to be a nun. Now, I had my high school sweetheart and our two perfect to us children. We decided no matter what, we were going to make it and things were going to be okay. Going through hard times just makes you enjoy and savor each day; precious moment by precious moment.

We learned we had to make our little family a priority and after two years of horrible medical care, we attended Bearskin Meadow Camp in California. We learned there were better options for treatment and care. We learned about clinical studies and trials we could be in to advance technology to work toward a cure and we learned about how to LIVE and THRIVE not just survive with Type 1 Diabetes. For us, that meant that we could no longer live and work in the place we loved near family. We had to choose between moving to California or Missouri where there were similar studies, better climate, and better doctors for our son. In the end, Missouri and a country setting was our decision for our quality of life and we are working toward making that home every day. We did not choose THIS path, but it was the one set before us. By learning to embrace "the sweet life" of being a Type 1 family instead of trying to avoid it, we are all doing better, day by day.

One of the toughest things I had to accept was that I physically did not fit into a 9-5 life anymore. Since I am the one who gets up with Wyatt in the night, I have to work around those constant hard nights. I don't get consistent sleep I need at night, so I have to find a way to nap during the day.

I had always taught in either traditional or online classrooms and was not used to being with so few people all day. After I had my first book published and finished my Master of Arts in Teaching/Teacher Leadership, I decided to dedicate my time to helping other people thrive, not just survive in this life. Through working as a couple doing writing, art, educational consulting, training, and coaching, it allows us to be available for our son's needs, home school our children, travel, and have a more flexible schedule.

We still participate in studies and have to go to routine doctor's appointments every three months, so God seemed to have this design for our life in mind when he sent us our son. After we embraced all of this, things immediately started falling into place. I am a passionate educator with years of professional experience, so it makes sense that I would be able to continue to do that on line, in person, and in a virtual format. Always having loved art, designing, and illustrating, it makes sense that I am able to write, illustrate my books, and also design training programs and educational resources to share globally. I am so grateful for opportunities to help, inspire, and encourage others.

It all boiled down to embracing our new life, making a decision to thrive, not just survive the changes, and now that we were set up for success, we needed to dial back in our own health. Grief weight, moving, stress, anxiety over family illnesses, deaths, and change in our lives definitely took its toll on us. Now that we had given our son his best chance for a healthy full life, we needed to do the same thing for ourselves. Step by step, we were getting our life back on track! We had managed the transition to Missouri, our new doctors were great, we were making wonderful friends, and our hearts were healing. We were ready for the next chapter of thriving as a Type 1 Family, not just surviving.

#Lesson 17: Thrive, don't just survive!

Reflection Opportunity:

Think about a time in your life when you thought you just couldn't go on. What did you do to help yourself out of that emotional slump? Were you able to see how God had a better plan for you? Did you have anyone in your life who stepped in and helped you out? Take some time to write down those memories and let go of anything that is still holding you back.

You were made to thrive, not just survive in this life! You can be more and do more with your life if you can take the time to identify what you need and want to do, then put your plan into place! Share your thoughts on my Facebook author page: Trina Licavoli Gunzel or keep them in your notebook to refer to later and see how far you have progressed.

Chapter 18

Losing The Grief Weight And Stabilizing Your Life: The PIE Diet

I was eating lunch with some of my girlfriends and listening to all of the diets they had been trying and how unsuccessful they had been. Many of them didn't have much energy, they didn't feel that they could continue the diet they were on, or had tried, and the same feeling of hopelessness was mixed between menu orders that looped back to the same old or minimal results. I had shared some tips that were actually working for me and it wasn't really seen as something anyone could fully grasp.

After listening to all of the comments and needs of my friends, I finally said, "I have found the most amazing diet that actually works! It has changed my life! I'm down four dress sizes, have lost over twenty pounds, and I have more energy than ever! It's called the PIE diet!" Everyone laughed and said if there was a PIE diet, they would try that so…I am going to share it with you! If you embrace the PIE diet, you can feel better, look better, make better choices, and use your amazing brain to think better about what you are doing to get the results you want. Yes, you truly can have all the PIE you want, and look and feel amazing! I'm going to give you the blueprint for success that you can build on. Enjoy!

When I think about my favorite kind of PIE, I think I would choose sour cream cherry pie. Really, I enjoy fresh pies with seasonal fruit, but I am not sure I have ever met a PIE I didn't like. Moving to the Midwest for better doctors and climate for my Type 1 Diabetic son, I found myself bombarded with new and exciting PIE choices at almost every restaurant we frequented in our new surroundings. I had lost both of my in-laws to cancer, moved completely away from all of my family and closest friends, and was searching for anything familiar and comforting. Before I knew it, PIE was my new favorite comfort food.

Somehow, over the next couple years, I managed to transition from some version of myself I had recognized to fifty pounds overweight and didn't really see any signs of stopping. I had to realize that my comfort PIE was actually hurting me, and turn it into something that would help me instead. When I was able to see the PIE for what it needed to be, my life started to drastically change for the better. I know that if other people can see their favorite PIE as Physical exercise, Intentional eating, and Eight hours of sleep, they will be able to get the results they want too. It seems simple, but the best things in life usually are. I am going to show you how to think better so you get the results you want in the way it works for you. After all, YOU are the only one who can actually change your circumstances and when you see what you need to do, you are empowered to change. Let's get started enjoying the PIE!

Over the years, you might put on a few pounds and think that it's no big deal. However, when you combine holiday binges with a lack of sleep and little to no exercise, you are putting a system into place that is due to fail. There have been a lot of technology advances we have been a part of through clinical trials and studies with our son, and they have resulted in a better quality of life, especially in the sleep department.

I had no idea how detrimental a lack of sleep can be but! However, as any Type 1 Diabetic parent can attest to, there are many nights and years of checking your child for low blood sugar. Checking routinely at midnight and that early morning window, especially after high exercise or questionable carb counting, sick days, and more, adds up to a lot of sleepless nights. We are presently using a combination of some helpful technology that results in more continuous hours of sleep for all of us, most of the time.

Our son wears a Medtronic pump and cgm (continuous glucose monitor). These two devices work with a monitor called a Sentry that I have by my night table. I am able to see and hear any alarms that my son's pump may have in the night. The benefit of the pump/cgm combination is that his blood sugar shows up in real time and there is a minute by minute graph with data tracking low and high blood sugar trends. Alarms can be set to sound at a specific number so that, for example, if low blood sugar glucose is predicted, intervention can happen before severe low blood sugar takes place.

With our newest model pump, there is even a built in suspend feature so that when our son does go low overnight, the pump will actually stop giving him insulin for two hours, which results in his blood sugar coming back up. This is life saving technology we have used and our son hasn't had a low blood sugar seizure since he has been using it. I am sharing all of this because SLEEP is very underrated. When we don't get enough sleep, we are tired, we can't make good decisions, we are more prone to infections, and our overall well being is affected. I really underplayed how much weight gain was attributed to a lack of that quality "REM" sleep, but getting up every two hours for years had me feeling like I was living in a fog.

By taking control of my life, and putting back into practice those tried and true things that really work, I was able to start reversing the numbers. Never in my life did I ever need or want to lose 20 pounds let alone 50. I knew my weight was just going to continue to go up so I just decided to step by step start reversing the numbers. It is really a mental shift to take care of yourself and I could see how putting JUST my son first had really taken its toll on my own health. Let me break down each piece of this PIE concept for you.

PIE INGREDIENTS

Every great pie starts with specific ingredients. If you add too much or too few of something, you won't actually create the desired PIE you want, right? If you aren't a baker, but you enjoy eating PIE you order, just picture the best version of a slice of PIE you've eaten and compare it to one of your least favorite versions. It is obvious there are different flavors, textures, and overall quality to the product that gives us the desired taste we are looking for. If we apply this same thinking to ourselves, how can we create the best version of ourselves? How can we be the PIE that we desire? Let's look at the first basic ingredient, remember, we are keeping this simple. Let's look at the P in PIE. Alone, it's just the letter P, right? It's also the first letter in something we crave and want for and in our physical self. The P stands for PHYSICAL EXERCISE. I am starting with that because we have to stop making excuses for why we can't do something and focus more on what we CAN do.

I want you to use this included Personal Design Plan I've created for you to help yourself see how you can get an A+ for yourself in life. If we can identify the need, then we can think of ways to change it.

Let's start right now with just this simple rating scale. Look at yourself right now and take a personal life assessment. I am going to have you write down and rate very specific things so you create a baseline of data for YOURSELF. Congratulations! YOU are starting the best work for YOURSELF you will ever do! Grab a pen or pencil and let's get started.

Personal Design Plan for An A+ Life For:

Present Life Report Card: Date:

Rate your life on the grading scale with A+ being the best it could ever be and an F being the worst it could be. Circle the appropriate letter as it applies to your situation. (Make copies if you want to see your progression and grade yourself again over time.)

1. Your present personal weight for YOU:

   A+ B C D F

2. Fulfillment in relationships with others:

   A+ B C D F

3. Happiness with your work: A+ B C D F
4. Time spent doing your hobbies: A+ B C D F
5. Quality time spent with your kid(s). (If applicable) A+ B C D F or Not Applicable
6. Time spent with your pet(s). (If applicable)

   A+ B C D F or Not Applicable

7. Time spent on your health exercising:

   A+ B C D F

8. Time spent on your health eating intentionally:

   A+ B C D F

9. Quality time spent by yourself: A+ B C D F
10. Time spent in nature: A+ B C D F
11. Time spent renewing your spiritual side/faith/inner peace: A+ B C D F

12. Having a schedule that works for your life:

    A+ B C D F

13. Feeling like you are living your purpose:

    A+ B C D F

14. Ability to provide for yourself and your family:

    A+ B C D F

15. Time spent helping others: A+ B C D F

16. The overall grade you would give your present life: A+ B C D F

17. The grade you think your Creator/God/Higher Power would give you: A+ B C D F

18. The way you want to be remembered:

    A+ B C D F

Congratulations on taking The Personal Design Plan for An A+ Life Assessment. You have taken the first step toward identifying areas in your life that you want to change. Once we know which areas we struggle with and OWN that, we can see it and work on changing. The great thing is, this change can happen as quickly as you want it to! Let's start right now!

Pick one thing on your list you really want to focus on today, and start there. Watch your life change as you reassess yourself over the next few weeks. Work to balance and restore areas of deficiencies. It is impossible to do them all at once. I am not asking you to burn yourself out and be perfect in every single area of your life. What I am concerned about is your end game. Is what you are doing today, tomorrow, in the future, going to get you the results that you want to have at the end of your life? Are you satisfied with the way you are living your life? If not, do the work it takes to change it. Be that change for YOURSELF!

It is so empowering to see, as we look introspectively, what our own true needs are. Without the distraction of other people's needs, we can see which areas of our life we have let go of and see how it has affected us. It is with the best of intentions that we care for others, try to help people, and take care of all of our responsibilities, but if we forget to take care of ourselves, we end up having nothing left to give and can become resentful and depressed.

I wanted to share this PIE diet because I see the things people want in life and I see the ways we punish ourselves through things like comfort food, addictions, staying up too late, arguing, and other numerous ways that drain our energy. By establishing routines, expectations for ourselves, and a way to focus our attention in a positive way, we actually end up getting more energy by doing

MORE! It sounds crazy right? How can we possibly get more energy by doing MORE? I hope this is helpful as you put what you've learned about yourself into practice in your own life. In order to be there for others, we must take care of ourselves.

#Lesson 18: What can you control?

Reflection Opportunity:

Grief can be overwhelming at times, but it helps to remember the things you can control. Start with just one. You can control brushing your teeth today. You can control eating something today. You can control the smile or frown you choose to wear today. Find a way to win, TODAY!

Make a plan for one area of your life you want to improve. Start there and build! With each step, you are making progress toward where you want to be in life, but you must continue taking those little steps. Write down your thoughts in the personal notebook you've been creating or, share your thoughts on my Facebook author page: Trina Licavoli Gunzel.

Chapter 19

Bloopers: The Comical and Horror Stories of Type 1 Diabetes

This section of my life continues to be added to on a daily basis. This is the part where we get to laugh at the craziness of it all and see that we can all relate to these comical and horror moments in life. Enjoy as you laugh, cringe, smile, cry, and experience the Type 1 Family life.

Have you ever went out to a restaurant, pulled out a large syringe, and had half the room look at you in horror like you are a drug addict? Then, wait for it, instead of injecting yourself, you reach over and pull up the sleeve and skin of your child and inject your four year old son behind his arm. The horror faces turn to sympathetic shocks and you hear, "Oh, that poor boy!"

Have you ever been so tired that you could barely function? Yet, you are making lunch for your children. You had already helped your son check his blood sugar and went over and calculated what you needed to give him for his insulin dose. In the meantime, he gets up and goes to the bathroom. So, when you go to give the insulin shot, you find yourself looking at a child in their high chair shaking their head at you.

As you try to give them the insulin shot, you think to yourself, "How do I ever give this child a shot when they are moving so much?" Horrified, you drop the insulin filled syringe to the ground, realizing in your tired brain fog, you almost just killed your NON diabetic baby who does NOT need an insulin shot! I know that is the day I called my husband and my virtual teaching principal and told them I had to quit my online teaching job. I could not be the mother of a Type 1 Diabetic child, a new baby, and work all night and day without having serious problems happen. The lack of sleep was a huge issue. Everyone understood that this super mom had her limits.

Have you ever been woken up in the night with the feeling that you just had to go in and check on your child? I have had that happen many times, especially since my son was diagnosed. One night, I was really tired, and didn't want to get up, although there was a tug on my heart to go. After about ten minutes of debating it, I finally half woke up and tried to go out of my bedroom door.

Usually, I leave our door open so I can just quietly go out and not wake up my husband. However, we had shut our door earlier and I hadn't remembered to open it. I walked in the dark straight into our door and smacked it so hard with my entire body. CRASH! It woke my husband and snapped me out of my middle of the night fog quickly. When I went into my son's room, I checked his pump and it had an error message saying "No insulin delivered." His pump had just stopped working in the night and when I checked his blood sugar, he was almost 500! My husband was awake anyway, so he helped me change out Wyatt's site and reset his pump. We also had to give him an insulin shot injection to get the insulin in his body more quickly. I am so thankful I listened to my heart or we would have been headed for a trip to the hospital in the morning with our son back in DKA.

Have you ever been out somewhere for an event and had your child leave their medical bag? We've been trying to give our son more responsibility and have him take ownership of his Diabetes. He was excited because he had been able to do an interview in Branson, Missouri with Yakov Smirnoff for a scouting project about the citizenship process. Apparently in his excitement, he left his bag at the theatre. We unfortunately didn't realize this until we had driven the 20 minutes home then asked him to check his blood sugar before he went to bed. There was no response at the theatre when I called, but fortunately, after my husband drove him back into town, they were able to find his medical "go bag." Those medical supplies are NOT optional and always have to be with him.

Have you ever arrived late at a hotel and made a decision like this? "Oh, it's just going to be a quick overnight stay, we don't need to bring in all of the medical supplies. Let's just take in the "go bag" with the blood glucose meter and we'll be fine." At 4 a.m., I heard alarms going off from my son's pump. When I went to check him, he had a high predicted alarm because, at some point in the night, he had ripped his site out of his leg and it kept going in and out of his skin. There was blood everywhere, it smelled like insulin, and he hadn't been getting insulin for an unknown amount of hours. That was it! Everyone was up, running to the car in the cold to get the medical supplies, we were doing site changes early, and since we weren't sleeping anymore, we just got back on the road. Good times I am thankful I can laugh about now. Not!

Have you ever tried to order something out that you feel might be a "healthy" option or just wanted to eat something "fun" and try something new? When you have done that, have you ever completely miscalculated the carbohydrate amount and then had to be up all night either chasing a low or high blood sugar? There are so many highs and lows of raising a Type 1 Diabetic child: emotionally, physically, and yes, actually, with blood sugar readings. When this happens, we have learned to be up checking blood sugar every 3 hours. If we don't our son either ends up really high or really low.

We were taught to check blood sugar before eating and dose for the carbohydrates at that time, too. Then, to eat at the following times, based on the reading: If the range is below 80, treat the low blood sugar. Eat/drink and wait 15 minutes, then check again and dose for the carbohydrates, minus 15 carbs from the total to treat the low. If the blood sugar range is 80-120, dose for the carbohydrates and then eat. If the blood sugar range is above 200, dose for the blood sugar (bolus) correction and carbohydrates, but wait 20 minutes to eat. If the blood sugar range is above 300, dose for the blood sugar (bolus) correction and carbohydrates, but wait 30 minutes before eating.

By dosing first then waiting to eat for a specific time when the blood sugar reading is high (out of your optimum range), it gives the insulin time to work in the body, meet the food intake, and get back into the target blood sugar range. Our target is 80-120, which is pretty tight, but we like to have a great goal to work toward. Depending on the day, blood sugar readings are like the weather, and ever changing, but, if our son had perfect blood sugar all the time, he wouldn't be a Type 1 Diabetic, would he?

Have you ever had a time using insulin shots where your blood sugar would spike from 40 to 400 in the same day? Our first two years living as a Type 1 Diabetic family were so frustrating. No matter what we did, we just couldn't seem to get our son's numbers to stabilize. Our doctor wouldn't let us adjust his formulas and we didn't understand the communication breakdown. We were using two different insulin types, had to give our son up to 8 injections a day and he was not growing. He was a very active kid and loved to swim. Our worst night with Type 1 since he was diagnosed, was two years into it.

We had been at a family party and he had been in and out of the pool swimming all day. We would have him get out every hour, check him, give him a snack and insulin and then he would swim again. This was during our two year period of only doing shots and while we weren't happy with the treatment, our doctor wouldn't let us get on a pump for our son.

At that time, the only way to know his blood sugar was to do a finger poke using a blood glucose meter kit. The challenge about that is, you only have points of data, you don't know if blood sugar is going high or low and so you can't intervene. This usually results in drastic spiking which can cause mini seizures that might look like your child "spacing out" and occasionally wetting their pants. That day was just a fun day for everyone else, but for us, it meant estimating a lot of "unknown" carbohydrate filled foods, trying to monitor exercise, and then checking him before we put him to bed. Wyatt's blood sugar was around 400 after he had eaten cake and been swimming all day so we did our regular routine of his nighttime insulin shot with his blood glucose correction. We hadn't had much training on the long term effects of exercise, especially swimming, which can result in low blood sugar as much as 24 hours later.

At midnight, everyone was fine when I went to feed our little baby girl. At 4am, I thought I heard my daughter crying, but when I went to her room, she was still sleeping. I opened my son's door to find him crying, rolling on the floor, in a full blown seizure. His clothes were wet and he couldn't talk. His mouth was clenched and he looked absolutely terrified. I ran out to get his blood sugar kit and called my husband.

We were just about ready to give him a glucagon shot to bring him up from a severe low blood sugar, but when we checked, his blood glucose reading showed he was 78. The only thing that we could figure happened, was that his body went severely low in the night and induced a seizure as a last resort to save him. We called our local doctor and our endocrinologist at the closest major hospital, two hours away. One advised us to keep him quiet and calm at home if his blood sugar was in range, the other wanted us to bring him in. Because our son was terrified and didn't even recognize us for six hours, we decided to just keep him quiet at home and comfort him. We put him in clean clothes, prayed for him, wrapped him in his favorite blanket and just held him on the sofa for the day. After he stopped seizing, his entire left side of his body wasn't working. He couldn't walk, his left arm was bent up almost like a claw and he wasn't talking at all. In this state of fear and not recognizing anyone, he would panic if anyone other than his dad went near him and he didn't want to move.

We decided to just give him some time, kept checking his sugar, and since he was in range and didn't have anything else wrong, we decided to wait. After that long quiet day, it was a miracle when our son, after six hours, finally relaxed and said, "Hi guys, I'm back!" He tells us now that he just felt so scared and couldn't get out of his body. He was trapped inside and didn't have a way to tell us he was hurt or going low. I hope nobody else ever has to go through that. We were so thankful when we were able to get a new doctor and get switched to a pump and cgm because, while they have their own issues, we have not had any seizures or severe low blood sugars that required using a glucagon gun ever, and we still have our son, praise God!

A heart to heart message: As parents, we always try to do the best for our children, but sometimes even our best intentions need altering. Listen, keep trying, and most of all, show love. This is a little excerpt I'm sharing called - The story of two tuck-ins and two kisses: Once there was a little boy who had been living with Type 1 Diabetes for seven years. His mom would quietly go into his room every night and check his blood sugar, trying not to wake him. After having to poke his little finger to get a blood glucose reading and calibrate his insulin pump, she would give him an extra kiss on his cheek and tuck him in again. Usually, she would just turn off the light and go back to bed, trying to do all this as quietly as possible, so as not to wake him or his little sister.

One day, his little sister said, I wish I had Type 1 Diabetes, too. When her mother asked her why, she said this: "Every night, I hear you check on my brother, and I know he gets all the extra tuck-ins and kisses. I wish I had Type 1 Diabetes because I am missing out on all that extra love." So now, every night, there are two extra tuck-ins and two extra kisses, no matter how many times the mommy has to check blood sugars, and two extra sweet children never have to feel they are shorted on love again. Win, win. Love is the present day cure, because life doesn't wait. Enjoy those sweet, extra, intentional moments. With love, Trina Licavoli Gunzel.

#Lesson 19: The highs and lows of raising a Type 1 Diabetic child!

Reflection Opportunity:

Do you raise a Type 1 Diabetic child or know someone who does? Do you have Type 1 Diabetes yourself? You are not alone in this! I hope that be reading and being able to share in some of our highs and lows over the years with this, you feel more connected. I wish so badly when I was sitting in the hospital with my son, I could have read something like this to know what I was really going to go through and see that it was going to be possible. So many times I wished I had a resource like this to give to others so they would understand what my day to day life had been changed to and show me some compassion and understanding.

Have you thought of anything while reading this that you want to remember or share with someone else? I would love to connect with you and hear your Type 1 high and low experiences. By sharing with others, we can better understand and put a personal side to Type 1 Diabetes that I hope will result in a cure. In so many ways, my prayer is that this book really helps people connect with that personal side and the 24-7 Type 1 life. I'd love to hear your stories! Write them in your notebook so you can see how far you've come. It is all part of the journey! Share your thoughts on my Facebook author page: Trina Licavoli Gunzel.

Chapter 20

How To Keep Your Marriage; In Good Times And In Bad

I could write a whole book and teach many workshops on this, but I just want to share a few very specific tips to keep in mind as you are going through any struggle that strains your marriage:

1. Remember your vows.

2. Reread your vows.

3. Realize you signed up for this.

4. Remember that you love each other.

5. Hold on to the promises you made to each other on your wedding day.

6. Find your vows and reread them, yes, it's actually all in there!

7. Make time for each other.

8. Never forget your first love, long before kids, long before financial struggles, long before any sickness came into the picture…hold on to that for as long as you can, then hold on some more.

9. The cutest old forever love couple I've ever heard shared, "Don't ever go to bed angry, stay up and fight!" Whatever life throws your way, you are stronger than you know. Fighting doesn't mean things are over, but sometimes it takes a good argument (or many) in order to grow.

10. In case you can't find yours…reread this often:

I promise to love you in good times and in bad, in sickness and in health, for rich or for poor…(many versions here, for all of time and eternity, until death do us part…)…I would love to add: and to always remember that you were first my friend before you were my spouse and to always treat you accordingly, with all the love, kindness, and respect I hold for you in my heart.

Not to overdo it but…yes, I want to overdo it: Read your vows. If you both hold up your end of the bargain, you will make it through ANYTHING life throws your way, together. My greatest mentor who ever walked this earth modeled love, kindness, forgiveness, and compassion. It seems that when we feel we have given all we can give, we can always do more.

#Lesson 20: What are you afraid that you can't make it through in your marriage?

Reflection Opportunity:

I have found that when we harbor fears, they built up and can ultimately, destroy anything we are trying to do. We can be such victims to our self sabotaging behaviors, ideas, addictions, thoughts, and actions. Why not just pull them out into the open and look them straight in the face to take away the fear?

I always thought the worst thing that could ever happen to me in my marriage would be for my husband to cheat on me. In our early years, I just flat out told my husband that if he ever did, I would divorce him, period. He, on the other hand, told me that no matter whatever happened between us, divorce was not an option. Period. Now thankfully, we have not ever experienced that, but we have experienced LOTS of other things and our relationship has definitely been strained and tried.

We have been high school sweethearts since we were 15, have been married over 18 years as I'm writing this, and we have had a lot of growing up to do together. I am looking forward to helping more marriages and doing workshops for couples, but this book is really about addressing the highs and lows of raising a Type 1 Diabetic child. For us, that in itself strained us (and does on a daily basis) in ways we never thought possible.

We have never been this tired, had to face almost financial bankruptcy because of the unimaginable costs, and had to completely overhaul every aspect of our life to accommodate this life threatening condition. I know it takes us constant, consistent effort to keep our marriage going strong and we have absolutely struggled but, I like to think we are stronger and better for it.

That's not always easy to see from the outside, but I can feel it and I see it reflected in my children. In addition to the vows, my other thought I want to leave you with is to stop wasting time. Don't waste time arguing, giving the silent treatment, building up rage and resentment or trying to play mental games and put guilt trips on each other. Strengthen your communication skills, build your listening skills, share laughter and memories to continue to build and grow your relationship and bring new ideas to your marriage to keep it fresh.

What ideas or impressions do you get from this chapter? You are welcome to share them on my Facebook author page: Trina Licavoli Gunzel. Feel free to also e-mail me at trina@trinagunzel.com for additional marriage workshop information and custom training. I pray for all marriages daily and want to lift your relationship up, whatever stage it is in. Grow, forgive, love, and enjoy each other. Amen.

Chapter 21

The Chapter Every Newly Diagnosed Type 1 Diabetic Needs To Know!

Some very specific, practical, and helpful ways to manage Type 1 Diabetes:

If you are reading just the first and last chapters of this book, I am glad you're here. If you want to really know more about the highs and lows of raising a Type 1 Diabetic child and understand that experience, please read the rest of the book. However, if you have come here for just the bulleted list and some tips, I'm going to give them to you. You also found the bonus section of the book with original song lyrics to encourage and inspire you so I hope you enjoy those as well.

Here you go. The Top 7 List Newly Diagnosed Type 1 Diabetic Needs To Know: (I'm including 7 since my son has been living Type 1 Strong now for 7 years)

1. Do whatever you have to do to get the best care for yourself. For us, that meant moving. For us, that meant participating in studies and asking all of our questions until we felt trained and confident. You are your best advocate! Make sure you understand what you need to #thrive not just survive living with diabetes.

2. Really know how to manage sick days. Keep the training brochure they give you in the hospital and all of those emergency numbers on your refrigerator so you can get the care and help you need when you need it most.

3. Make a "go bag" you take with you wherever you go that has the life saving supplies you need. Our "go bag" includes: A glucagon pen, back up insulin, syringes in case our pump goes down, backup batteries, extra tape for sites, 15 carb juice boxes and snacks, extra test strips, a blood glucose monitor, an emergency contact number, bandages, and extra site change supplies. *(Add anything else you need)

4. Have some kind of support team: friends, family, church, sports, whoever – have "your people" that you can talk to and who will be your "family" to help you through this. It is a marathon, not a race and you will need people to help you with your child

that you can train. Everyone needs a date night now and then, even Type 1 parents. If you have Type 1 Diabetes, train your friends to help you so that if you are all out and you go unconscious, they will know how to save your life. It is great to have other people know how to use your glucagon pen; it just might save you!

5. Check your supplies and make sure they are current. Try to get some back up supplies stocked up so you aren't just living prescription refill to prescription refill. Also, change your sites often, especially if you notice you are having high blood sugars and don't know why. We have had sites bruise or get infected under the needle and our son wasn't getting his insulin. We rotate sites between his arms, legs, stomach and hips and this helps keep fresh tissue and allow site spots to heal.

6. Attend some kind of camp or training as soon as you can after you are diagnosed. I cannot say enough good things about The Diabetic Youth Families (Foundation) and Camp Bearskin Meadow in California. It honestly changed our life. We went to the family camp twice and made lifelong friends that only bonding through camp made possible. To get to spend quality time with other families and camp staff who really "get" what you're going through and live it 24-7 while getting the best training possible, really helps. I will always be grateful to our Grandma Alma who saw how much we were struggling and helped contribute to us getting to camp. There's no place like it!

7. Pray continuously. My faith is my rock and I wouldn't have made it through this otherwise. When everything seems dark and you feel it is too hard, you truly know you are not alone and there are much bigger struggles that have happened and still come out victorious. I will pray for you and I hope you are encouraged.

Along with the very specific, practical, and helpful ways to manage Type 1 Diabetes, I wanted to end with a very heart to heart message. I have overcome and won my own struggle with grief and depression because of my son getting diagnosed and almost losing him to Type 1 Diabetes. I know how much it hurts to see your loved ones suffer and not understand why these things are happening to them and you. I have a personal testimony and love that can only come from a deep faith relationship. I know my Savior lives and He is my rock, my redeemer, and my comforter.

Early on in my son's diagnosis, I would be woken up in the night with songs that came to me. These songs are from my heart and inspired by the only thing I can attribute them to, the comfort of the Holy Spirit. I was literally jolted awake on different nights to check Wyatt's blood sugar and given these songs that I had to write down as quickly as they showed up in my heart. I would not list my first profession as being a Christian songwriter and yet, that is exactly what was put on my heart for me to be and share. These songs are not just mine; they were made to encourage everyone. This book, this life, this whole process is so much bigger than my little family or I. We really hope and pray to be a light of hope and encouragement for others who struggle living with Type 1 Diabetes on a daily basis. There are so many battles everyone is silently fighting and I want to give a voice to this one, in hopes to spread awareness, love, and praise for all those working for a cure and helping people thrive, today!

Please enjoy these songs from my heart to yours. I hope to add links to them when they are recorded you can access from my website: www.trinagunzel.com. You'll be able to listen to them on-line, play them, sing along, shout them out, and know that you are not alone in this struggle. Dare to dream and live another day! Thank you for sharing your time and heart with me. You were made to #thrive not just survive in this life and I look forward to hearing of your successes and struggles as we encourage one another. *Welcome to the Dare To Dream Virtual Music Tour* to inspire and encourage you. I would love to hear you singing them and hear of how these lyrics inspire you. You are not alone!

#Lesson 21: #Love!

Reflection Opportunity:

If anything in this book touched your heart, spoke to you, or helped you understand the 24-7 life of a Type 1 family a little better, I would love to hear from you! Please interact with me and write a review on Amazon so others will find this book, today! Write down your thoughts and ways you can apply what you've learned to your life. Think of ONE person you know who might benefit from reading Can't Dia.beat.us and please share it with them. Every act of love makes a difference and we can help others through our positive direct influences and choices.

I look forward to connecting with you on my Facebook author page: Trina Licavoli Gunzel. Thank you for writing a review and sharing your Type 1 experiences or struggles you have overcome! There are so many highs and lows in this life, but we are stronger, together! #THRIVE!

Dare to Dream

Written by Trina Gunzel © 2015

Sometimes you may feel

That God's abandoned you.

And at every turn

You don't know what to do.

But that's when you have

Got to hold on tight,

Knowing God's the One with

Power to make it right.

Dare to dream until tomorrow.

Live to fight another day.

Dare to dream until tomorrow.

Face any challenge as you pray.

Look and see all the

Talents you possess

Made in the image of
The Lord's righteousness.
He's the One who sent
His son Jesus Lord,
Just to prove to you how
Much you are adored.

Dare to dream until tomorrow.
Live to fight another day.
Dare to dream until tomorrow.
Face any challenge as you pray.

So take this time
To focus on God's plan.
Praise him, reach out
And hold onto his hand.
As you focus on the
Blessings in your life;

Knowing he is holding

You, in times of strife.

Dare to dream until tomorrow.

Live to fight another day.

Dare to dream until tomorrow.

Face any challenge as you pray.

God's Team

Written by Trina Gunzel © 2015

It is all of God's creation
And it sweeps across the nation
In the city, in the street,
In somebody new that you meet.

It's the chance to help your neighbor.
Be a servant to the Lord.
If in God we trust means somethin'
Don't leave your talents unexplored.

We are better than we've been.
We are smarter than we know.
Take this chance to honor him.
Help our world heal and grow.

I need you and you need me,
Brothers sisters one and all.
Help me up; pray for me,
I'll pray for you; don't let me fall.

If we work together team,
We are stronger than divided.
If we glorify his name,
Through his love we are united.

Find a need, fill a need.
God made you just the way you are.
Do it all in honor of him
It may be close it may be far.

We are not givin' up!
We're here to fight the good fight!
Put your words into action
To help make the wrongs, right.

(Repeat song)

Take this chance to honor him.

Help our world heal and grow.

Take this chance to honor him.

Help our world heal and grow.

Faith

Written by Trina Gunzel © 2015

There is something
We cannot see;
Inside of you,
Inside of me.

It keeps us going
When we're down;
Makes us smile
When we want to frown.

Let me spell it,
Then you'll see,
The letters that are
Such a part of me.

F is for the friends I know

A is always trying to grow

I for inspiration that I need

T today and every day

H to heaven I lift my voice in praise.

Faith – it is believin.'

Faith – in somethin' without seein.'

Faith – sends the Holy Spirit.

Faith – in that instinct feelin.'

Faith – is always knowin.'

Faith – that Jesus Christ is lovin.'

Faith – you the way you are.

Faith – don't you have a little

FAITH!

God sent his son

To save the world.

Make him proud
By takin' care

Of his creation
And your fellow man.
Realize your part
Of a bigger plan!

Don't be selfish
And play the fool
Always remember
The golden rule.

F is for the friends I know
A is always trying to grow
I for inspiration that I need
T today and every day
H to heaven I lift my voice in praise.

Faith – it is believin.'

Faith – in somethin' without seein.'

Faith – sends the Holy Spirit.

Faith – in that instinct feelin.'

Faith – is always knowin.'

Faith – that Jesus Christ is lovin.'

Faith – you the way you are.

Faith – don't you have a little

FAITH!

What Do You Want From Me?

Written by Trina Gunzel © 2015

What do you want from me, Lord?
I'm here, but I'm fallin.'
What do you want from me, God?
I cannot hear your calling.

What do you want from me, Lord?
I used to think I saw your plan,
But, what do you want from me, God?
How much pain can one heart stand.
Just what do you want from me?

No matter what I try
It just keeps comin' apart
I don't know why.
Sometimes, I just feel
Like I need to scream
Or shout

Just what's going on
What's my life
Supposed to be about?
What do you want from me?

What do you want from me, Lord?
I'm here, but I'm fallin.'
What do you want from me, God?
I cannot hear your calling.

What do you want from me, Lord?
I used to think I saw your plan,
But, what do you want from me, God?
How much pain can one heart stand,
Just what do you want from me?

All I am is just me, God
And all I have, is faith in you, Lord.

My rock has been shaken
By this road, Lord, but
Not my, not my, not my
Faith in you!

So, what do you want from me, Lord?
I'm here, but I'm fallin.'
What do you want from me, God?
I cannot hear your calling.

What do you want from me, Lord?
I used to think I saw your plan,
But, what do you want from me, God?
How much pain can one heart stand,
Just what do you want from me?

I will dust, myself off
And shake off the burdens
Of yesterday's loss.

And put on my shield
Of your love and sacrifice
To get me through
Another tomorrow and
I know you will show me the way
When I pray.

What do you want from me, Lord?
I'm here, but I'm fallin.'
What do you want from me, God?
I cannot hear your calling.

What do you want from me, Lord?
I used to think that I saw your plan,
But, what do you want from me, God?
How much pain can one heart stand,
Just what do you want from me?

We Celebrate

Written by Trina Gunzel ©2015

We celebrate His life

We appreciate His death

Because through His sacrifice

Jesus saved us.

We celebrate His works

We appreciate His choice

Because through His sacrifice

Jesus saved us.

It is time for you and me

To face a new reality

Recommit our lives to honor

Why Jesus saved us.

Try a new way every day

Through our actions and how we pray

To make a difference in the world

Because Jesus saved us…

Because Jesus saved us…

Because Jesus saved us:

We can change our life

Because Jesus saved us:

We can reject sin

Because Jesus saved us:

We can honor him

Because
Jesus
saved
us…

Check out my website: www.trinagunzel.com for updated resources, books, and information. Thank you and I look forward to hearing from you. Connect on Facebook: Trina Licavoli Gunzel, Author Page.

Resources

This is the website for the camp information. Camp Bearskin Meadow Family Camp changed our life. We learned so much about how to manage Type 1 Diabetes NOW and got the real day to day help, training and understanding we desperately needed when our son was first diagnosed. I only wish we would have known about them earlier! We attended after struggling for two years but I want to share their information so you can learn about their amazing events, donate to their great organization, and get to camp and family events if you need to! Thank you DYF!

http://www.dyf.org/

5167 Clayton Road, Suite F
Concord CA 94521
p 925-680-4994
f 925-680-4863
email: info@dyf.org

The DYF (Diabetic Youth Families) Mission is: To improve the quality of life for children, teens and families affected by diabetes. The organization provides education and recreation within a supportive community, encouraging personal growth, knowledge and independence.

The JDRF has many events, fundraising campaigns, funds clinical trials, improves technology, and is working toward a cure for Type 1 Diabetes! Look for regional JDRF events near you!

http://jdrf.org/

The JDRF is the leading global organization funding Type 1 Diabetes research. Around the world, millions of people live with Type 1 Diabetes. It is a life-threatening autoimmune disease that affects both children and adults. Presently, there is no way to prevent it, and no cure. JDRF works every day to support, partner, and fun research for a cure. We have participated in JDRF funded studies and events. Thank you JDRF!

Find more information about Type 1 Diabetes from the American Diabetes Association at:

http://www.diabetes.org/living-with-diabetes/complications/ketoacidosis-dka.html?referrer=https://www.google.com/

Find additional information and resources at:

www.trinagunzel.com

www.jongunzel.com

www.type1family.com

About the Author

Petrina Licavoli Gunzel (Trina) is a professional and experienced educator with her B.S. in Elementary Education, and certifications in Early Childhood, Middle School Language Arts, ESL, and her Master of Arts in Teaching/Teacher Leadership. She works as an Educational Consultant, Trainer,

Teacher, and Author/Illustrator. She has worked throughout her career educating children and adults, with over 15 years of formal teaching and public speaking experience. She has been published with Scholastic in educational resources, materials, and through *Instructor Magazine*. Her first family keepsake book: *Grandmas Are Gorgeous* continues to be gifted and enjoyed by families and children and is sold anywhere books are sold online.

Trina lives with her husband who was her high school sweetheart and their two children, Wyatt and Abbie, near Branson, Missouri on their little family farm. They enjoy traveling, gardening, raising their pastured birds, and helping others be Type 1 strong.

Always having a passion for education and learning, Trina and her husband, Jon, work training individuals and groups. They create educational materials and resources for families. They have a heart for Type 1 Diabetics, a passion for marriages, and enjoy sharing, creating, and designing solutions to problems. You can contact them to schedule custom workshops to meet your needs.

Connect with Trina through social media and find her books anywhere books are sold online:

www.trinagunzel.com ww.trinagunzel.com/blog

Amazon: http://www.amazon.com/Trina-Licavoli-Gunzel/e/B00KD1XFKS

Twitter: @TrinaGunzelTrina

https://twitter.com/tgunzeltrina

Facebook Author Page: Trina Licavoli Gunzel

Like her Author Page for more information.

Instagram: Trinagunzel

Periscope: Trina Gunzel

Pinterest: https://www.pinterest.com/trinaauthor/

Find additional information and resources at:

www.jongunzel.com

www.type1family.com

Hire Trina Gunzel for Educational Training, Workshops, and Author's Events at: www.besteducators.com or www.trinagunzel.com or e-mail trina@trinagunzel.com

Thank you!

Trina Licavoli Gunzel

Notes

Notes

Made in the USA
Charleston, SC
27 November 2015